JÜRGEN HABERMAS

KEY SOCIOLOGISTS

Series Editor: PETER HAMILTON
The Open University, Milton Keynes

This series presents concise and readable texts covering the work, life and influence of many of the most important sociologists, and sociologically-relevant thinkers, from the birth of the discipline to the present day. Aimed primarily at the undergraduate, the books will also be useful to pre-university students and others who are interested in the main ideas of sociology's major thinkers.

MARX AND MARXISM
PETER WORSLEY, Professor of Sociology, University of Manchester

MAX WEBER
FRANK PARKIN, Tutor in Politics and Fellow of Magdalen College, Oxford

EMILE DURKHEIM
KENNETH THOMPSON, Reader in Sociology, Faculty of Social Sciences, The Open University, Milton Keynes

TALCOTT PARSONS
PETER HAMILTON, The Open University, Milton Keynes

SIGMUND FREUD
ROBERT BOCOCK, The Open University, Milton Keynes

C. WRIGHT MILLS
J. E. T. ELDRIDGE, Department of Sociology, University of Glasgow

THE FRANKFURT SCHOOL
TOM BOTTOMORE, Emeritus Professor of Sociology, University of Sussex

GEORG SIMMEL
DAVID FRISBY, Department of Sociology, University of Glasgow

KARL MANNHEIM
DAVID KETTLER, Professor of Political Studies, Trent University, Ontario; VOLKER MEJA, Associate Professor of Sociology, Memorial University of Newfoundland, and NICO STEHR, Professor of Sociology, University of Alberta

MICHEL FOUCAULT
BARRY SMART, Department of Sociological Studies, University of Sheffield

THE ETHNOMETHODOLOGISTS
WES SHARROCK and BOB ANDERSON, Department of Sociology, University of Manchester

ERVING GOFFMAN
TOM BURNS, Emeritus Professor of Sociology, University of Edinburgh

JÜRGEN HABERMAS
MICHAEL PUSEY, University of New South Wales, Australia

ROBERT K. MERTON
CHARLES CROTHERS, University of Auckland, New Zealand

JÜRGEN HABERMAS

MICHAEL PUSEY
Department of Sociology
University of New South Wales, Australia

ELLIS HORWOOD LIMITED
Publishers · Chichester

TAVISTOCK PUBLICATIONS
London and New York

First published in 1987 by
ELLIS HORWOOD LIMITED
Market Cross House, Cooper Street,
Chichester, Sussex, PO19 1EB, England
and
TAVISTOCK PUBLICATIONS LIMITED
11 New Fetter Lane, London EC4P 4EE

Published in the USA by
TAVISTOCK PUBLICATIONS
and ELLIS HORWOOD LIMITED
in association with METHUEN INC.
29 West 35th Street, New York, NY 10001–2291

British Library Cataloguing in Publication Data
Pusey, Michael
Jürgen Habermas. — (Key Sociologists).
1. Habermas, Jürgen
I. Title   II. Series
301'.092'4   HM22.G3H3/
Library of Congress CIP data available

ISBN 0–7458–0038–6 (Ellis Horwood Limited — Library Edn.)
ISBN 0–7458–0117–X (Ellis Horwood Limited — Student Edn.)

Phototypeset in Times by Ellis Horwood Limited
Printed and bound in Great Britain by Richard Clay Limited, Chichester, W. Sussex

Contents

For . . .

Kurt and Carla Wolff
Maria and Gyorgy Markus

Michael Pusey is Senior Lecturer in Sociology at the University of New South Wales in Sydney, Australia. He was educated first in England, then at the Sorbonne in Paris, and subsequently at the University of Melbourne. After taking his doctorate from Harvard University (1972) he worked as a public servant and then pursued his researches in the Research School of Social Sciences at the Australian National University in Canberra before moving to Sydney in 1978.

Dr Pusey has published articles on critical theory and on the sociology and politics of public policy, education, and organisation. His books include *The Dynamics of Bureaucracy,* (Wiley, 1976), and an edited collection, *Control and Knowledge*, (ANU, 1980). He is presently working on a project that relates modern theories of the State to his empirical sociological studies of higher public servants — this work will appear as a book (Cambridge UP) in 1988.

Editor's foreword

The contribution made by Habermas to the development of modern sociology is both an extension of 'Critical Theory', and a significant alternative to it. Whilst this may seem at first sight a contradictory statement, it does express the somewhat complicated nature of Habermas's role in contemporary social theory.

It is important here to note that Habermas has made a contribution in a field which is in effect much wider than that of professional sociology — for it encompasses social philosophy, the theory of knowledge and communication, marxism and, of course, sociological theory.

At one extreme, we find Habermas represented as the inheritor of a long and notable intellectual tradition — that established by the Frankfurt School (for a fuller account of Habermas's role in relation to this tradition, see *The Frankfurt School*, by Tom Bottomore, also in the 'Key Sociologists' series).

Habermas's connections to the Critical Theory of the Frankfurt School's principal protagonists — especially Horkheimer and Adorno — are, however, rather tenuous. Habermas certainly developed concerns of central interest to his predecessors — the critique of positivism, an emphasis on features of bourgeois ideology as expressed through philosophies of science — but his interests have taken him in an important sense away from marxism, and towards social science.

Whereas Adorno and Horkheimer maintained a somewhat haughty separation between their Critical Theory and the theories and work of professional sociology and the other social sciences, Habermas has been keener to engage with the central theoretical paradigms of modern social science. Thus, for an understanding of Habermas's approach to the rationalization process, to communicative action and to ideology and legitimation, we must look not just at Marx, but at Weber, at Freud, and at the apparent arch-enemy of Critical Theory, Talcott Parsons, as sources of Habermas's reflections on the conditions of modern and future society.

In this book, Michael Pusey has taken the work of Habermas and subjected it to a scrutiny which is both critical and interpretive. Many readers coming to Habermas for the first time find his style daunting, and the breadth of his frame of reference taxing. The great value of this most helpful approach to Habermas's work is that it is not at all a mere 'translation' of his theories into a more accessible form, but a critical engagement with their content, and with their promise as an alternative paradigm of social theory.

For perhaps the first time in a study of this type, Habermas's work is presented by Professor Pusey in a form which both captures the exciting challenge of its scope, and at the same time deals with the essential concepts of the Habermasian paradigm in a way which makes them transparent without any reduction in the richness of their meaning.

As with previous volumes in the '**Key Sociologists**' series, this book represents a critical introduction to the work of a significant modern sociologist — in this case, perhaps the most significant figure in contemporary social theory. Whilst there is no way in which Professor Pusey's study could be characterized as making Habermas's work 'easy', there can be no doubt that it is the best starting point from which to appreciate the scale and importance of this key sociological thinker.

Peter Hamilton

Preface and acknowledgements

Scarcely anyone would now challenge what other people have said many times about Habermas, namely that he is one of the most important figures in German intellectual life today and perhaps the most important sociologist since Max Weber. One can safely assign many years to the study of his writings because his works are fascinating in their own right and because, in reading Habermas, one learns a great deal from a range of classical authors, in several disciplines, whom he brings to life with astonishing brilliance and audacity. But let no one say that he is easy to read!

Indeed, Habermas is extremely difficult, especially for an English-speaking readership [1]. The difficulties are of an order that requires a moment's consideration of what is involved in this engagement with him and also of the choices that have to be made in introducing him in an accessible way.

In the first place, we are dealing with a man who is still only in his fifties, very much alive, enormously productive, and constantly revising his work in the light of criticisms that he deliberately seeks from other scholars in several disciplines. Debates with contemporaries are interspersed with reconstructions of his classical authors — Marx, Weber, Dilthey, Lukács, Freud, Mead, Durkheim, Parsons, and many others — whom Habermas treats as virtual 'dialogue partners'. This work, accumulated through many shifts and revisions over some twenty years, is now systematically presented in his latest attempt to lay out the outlines of a critical theory of society. His *Theory of Communicative Action* spreads, in two volumes, over some 1200 pages of difficult arguments [2]. In his preface Habermas tells us that all of this is just a preliminary (!) and then, in retrospect, after the thing has been published he confesses — somewhat accurately, but with typical humility — that the whole work is 'impossibly academic' [3]! Consider, further, that

Habermas has been steeped in the philosophical abstractions of his own esoteric German tradition and it is soon clear that we shall not have an easy time — indeed, to avoid unnecessary bitterness it is better that the faint-hearted should give up now.

With the introduction and the first chapter I have tried to orient the reader to the philosophical foundations and to the critical intention of Habermas's work. However, there is need for some further specific consideration of other constituents, not only because Habermas has deliberately tied his arguments so closely to his reconstructions of other authors, but also because his project advances on several different fronts at the same time. Accordingly, Chapter 2 offers three fairly self-contained discussions: his theory of social evolution; his debates about the interpretation of meaning as well as his concept of 'lifeworld' (*Lebenswelt*); and, perhaps most importantly, an outline of Habermas's reconstruction of Max Weber. Special attention is given in this chapter, as elsewhere, to his bold treatment of Weber not merely because I read Habermas, above all, as a 'left-Weberian', but for the more important reason that of all the 'reconstructions' this is, in my view, the best single key to the enormously elaborate foundation of his larger work. Since Habermas's own views are so inextricably tied to his bold reformulations of other authors one is forced to follow him into at least some of his reconstructions to get a feeling for the strength and character of his work. There are so many of these reconstructions that one has no choice but to do this selectively. I have stressed the Weberian strand and used it throughout the book as the key also to Habermas's treatment of Marx. However, the cost of taking this route is that I have not taken up other reconstructions, most notably of Durkheim, Mead and Parsons, whom other readers of Habermas may judge to be of greater or equal importance to Weber.

As we have said, Habermas is still writing very prolifically. His largest and most recent work, *The Theory of Communicative Action* is very new and it remains to be seen how it will be received, epecially in the English-speaking world. It would be unwise to look at twenty years of work through the single lens of these two volumes and it would also make Habermas even more inaccessible. For these and other reasons the strategy of this book is to follow a few major lines of development from his early work to the most recent. Chapter 3 deals with 'Communication and Action' from his first formulations of the 'ideal-speech situation' through to the 'linguistic turn' of his later work. Chapter 4 follows the development of his political sociology in much the same way. I have stressed the continuities and, for the most part, approached Habermas's work with the modest but still somewhat daunting aim of relating him to a new readership with little or no prior knowledge of him. Since Habermas is quite complicated enough as it is without asking the reader to cope with another set of baffles, filters and mirrors, I have kept my own criticisms and questions to a minimum.

Finally, a word about the problem of Habermas's abstract language. Many readers will be tempted to join the voices who curse and ask, 'Why can't this be said more simply?', 'What does it mean in plain English?'. The demand that Habermas should somehow come out from behind his smoke-screen of abstractions and give account of himself 'more simply' or in 'plain English' is understandable as a cry of frustration and impatience. But beyond this it has to be recognized as a secretly aggressive ploy. It asks Habermas to abandon arguments that are carefully cast and defended in his own language and tradition and then to surrender all his positions to the reductive theory language of traditional British empiricism — and of the analytic philosophy with which it is usually protected. The reader who wants to understand Habermas must slowly and carefully learn *his* theory language. Accordingly, I have not sought to avoid or to 'translate' his terminology. On the contrary, I have tried to use the vocabulary selectively and in a way that makes it accessible — the repetition of key notions and the constant use of inverted commas to mark the special meanings of his terms are some of the stylistic devices that are used for this purpose. The many problems that remain point to the wide gaps between his tradition and ours and are not at all the fault of Thomas McCarthy who, as everyone agrees, has introduced and translated Habermas's major works with extraordinary clarity and precision. I am extremely grateful for his indispensable help.

I should also like to thank Maria Markus for her perennial friendship and encouragement. Special thanks are due to Maria and George Markus and to Richard Bernstein for their detailed and extremely helpful critical comments on the whole manuscript. I would also like to thank Gianfranco Poggi, Johann Arnason, Gary Robinson, and Raul Pertierra for their comments on various slabs of an early draft. I am grateful for the friendship and encouragement of my colleagues in the School of Sociology at the University of New South Wales and no less grateful to the many students with whom I have studied Habermas and Critical Theory. I am especially glad to have the continuing friendship of some of those who have gone on to postgraduate studies — most notably Jennifer Wilkinson, Gary Robinson, Christine Crowe, Rachel McKay and Jocelyn Pixley.

Sydney   Michael Pusey
December 1986

NOTES

[1] See Habermas's interesting comments about this in, Jürgen Habermas, 'A Philosophical-Political Profile', *New Left Review*, **151**, pp. 75–105, 1985. He finds it easier to be heard in America than in Britain where, he says very politely, 'empiricism has become second nature' to the point he detects an 'estrangement in basic philosophical convictions' (p. 79).

[2] *Theorie des kommunicativen Handelns* (Frankfurt: Suhrkamp, 1981). Band I: *Handlungsrationalität und geselllschaftliche Rationalisierung*, 534 pp., Band II: *Zur Kritik der funktionalistischen Vernunft*, 633 pp.

[3] 'The Dialectics of Rationalisation: An Interview with Jürgen Habermas', Axel Honneth *et al.*, Telos, **49**.

Introduction

HABERMAS...

Jürgen Habermas, now in his late fifties (he was born in 1929), is a professor at the University of Frankfurt — in the same university that was the first home of the early Frankfurt School that has been such an important influence on his own intellectual development.

Since Habermas has a somewhat reserved and formal bearing, his personal and family life are not displayed for public attention and it is enough that we should know that he is married and that he has three children. His upbringing is more relevant to his intellectual work. In the English-speaking world we have now largely forgotten that a whole generation can be stamped by social and political traumas — that was true of an earlier generation of British and American intellectuals who knew the Great Depression of the early 1930s. Habermas and his generation of German intellectuals grew up in Nazi Germany. Habermas remembers [1]:

> At the age of 15 or 16, I sat before the radio and experienced what was being discussed before the Nuremberg Tribunal; when others, instead of being struck silent by the ghastliness, began to dispute the justice of the trial, procedural questions, and questions of jurisdiction, there was that first rupture, which still gapes. Certainly it is only because I was still sensitive and easily offended that I did not close myself to the fact of a collectively realized inhumanity in the same measure as the majority of my elders.

Habermas's radical commitments developed later, in the 1950s, and after a long training in his own classical German philosophical tradition. Yet, clearly his break with the insularity and provincialism [2] of German cultural life had its roots somewhere in the first consciousness of his adolescence and youth. His widening intellectual preoccupations soon pressed him into a study of American pragmatism and into other areas of philosophy that were not ordinarily part of the experience of his fellow German philosophy students among whom he began, despite his classical training, to feel like 'some kind of foreigner' [3]. He says that the electrifying influence of Adorno, to whom he was an assistant in 1956, had much to do with his own increasingly systematic 'sociological' and critical explorations of the same texts — of Marx, Freud, and others — that had so influenced the earlier Frankfurt School of some 25 years before him.

Habermas initially strongly supported the student radicals of the 1960s and distanced himself from them only when basic intellectual freedoms came under threat. He retains strong ties with a broad range of left social and intellectual movements. He recently addressed the Spanish Parliament and now lectures widely in North America and Europe.

From his writings and through his relationships with scholars, activists, and friends in several countries, Habermas has acquired a reputation as a man who is extraordinarily open to criticism. Although he admits to 'a certain stiffness' [4] he is obviously a person of great humility — he seems genuinely suprised by the attention he has received. For Habermas the intellectual life is not a game, or a career, or a cultivation of wit and taste, or even 'learning for learning's sake'. It is above all a vocation. One aspect of the man that permeates every aspect of the work is his ethical seriousness. The single purpose of the work is to anticipate and to justify a *better* world society — one that affords greater opportunities for happiness, peace, and community. Since Habermas is also a rationalist the *better society is the more rational society*, in short, a society that is geared to collective needs rather than to arbitrary power.

HIS CHALLENGE...

Habermas offers a comprehensive new social theory that is avowedly *critical* inasmuch as it challenges *both* the criteria on which the reader expects to judge this and every other social theory *and* the standards we use to accept, reject, or simply to interpret the everyday social world we inhabit.

English-language translations address a predominantly British and North American readership that is more or less comfortably committed to one of two perspectives towards society, economy, politics and letters. The first 'normal' or majority perspective is formed in its own philosophical and cultural inheritance of traditional empiricism. Here, in the British variant especially, there are no affinities with the German tradition. This tradition is therefore instinctively sceptical and wary of all 'grand theory' and 'metaphysics', and prone to view all strong concepts of Society, and all theoretically oriented sociology, as mischief and artifice, or at best, as *jeux d'esprit*. Habermas addresses also a second, minority readership that is committed, in a very different way, to some variant of orthodox marxism. For different reasons, this second perspective is set in the same inhospitable attitude to the German Enlightenment tradition from which Habermas writes.

Habermas means to persuade those of the majority that their grounds have failed and that, *faute de mieux*, they are left with an irrational individualism that is the at the root of all our troubles. Those in the minority perspective are challenged with the gentle accusation that they have not yet had the courage to re-work their philosophical foundations or to re-examine their view of modernity and that they are, for these reasons, stranded in a hopelessly discouraging apocalyptic nihilism.

Both perspectives are inadequate. Neither has grasped the 'suppressed traces of Reason' that provide the better groundings for a critical social theory of 'modernity'.

AND ITS CONTEXT

The challenge will be clearer if we are reminded of some of the basic contrasts between Habermas's own German intellectual tradition and the very different philosophical attitudes of the English-speaking readership. Three contrasts are of special importance.

'Weak' versus 'strong' concepts of reason

Since Kant and Hume there has been no real disagreement about the validity of the mathematical sciences or of the Newtonian physics that both philosophers understood in some depth. The contrasts and differences that have persisted originate instead from diverging understandings of the nature of science and of its relation to philosophy. In the British empiricist tradition, from David Hume to the present day, science is modelled on the methodologically and experimentally controlled application of procedures for the study of 'natural phenomena'. The aim is to explain empirical events and causal relations so as to better make 'Nature give up here secrets'. In this tradition, 'Nature' is easily generalized into a generic 'objective world' but, conversely, reasons are always particular; and indeed, the term 'reason' is normally reduced to refer only to a specific argument or inference properly framed in terms of the rules of evidence.

Although Habermas is no transcendental philosopher he certainly writes against the background of a tradition with a *strong generic concept of Reason* — with a capital 'R' [5]. In this tradition that has its roots in classical Greek philosophy and that stretches from Kant to Hegel and Marx. Reason is more commonly understood in this general way as the guide, the premise, the common ground, of all particular reasons. In the strongest Hegelian version that Marx inherited, Reason is the creative potentiality, not of the single individual but rather of a collective 'history-making subject' or 'species subject'. From this perspective it is natural to think of Science (with a capital 'S') and even of History (with a capital 'H') as the accomplishments of Reason, and of progress as a process of rationalization.

The individual versus the collective subject

Traditionally, in British (and American) social and political philosophy, and from Locke and Hobbes to the classical liberalism and utilitarianism of J. S. Mill and Jeremy Bentham, the individual has a clear primacy. The natural relation between one individual and the next is of difference and competition. Consequently individuals mutually contract to assign some of their natural rights to the State — so that they may more happily pursue their own individual ends. Only the private enterprise of the individual is creative.

On the other hand, in the German tradition from Hegel to Marx it is natural to think of the individual as an instance of a collective and even of a transcendental history-making subject. Indeed, German sociology grew out of historiscism and it was first conceived (*Völkerpsychologie*) as the (collective) psychology of the people (*Volk*), understood as a collective subject, and in the stronger Hegelian version, as a spiritual and cultural entity that transcends the individual.

'Weak' versus 'strong' concepts of society and state

Without too much exaggeration one can say that in the British empiricist tradition there is no Society with a capital 'S' but only an aggregation of individuals each pursuing his or her own 'private' benefit. Although of course in actuality there may be some consciousness of collective identity — in moments of crisis and patriotic sentiment — for the most part this tradition rejects all ontologically grounded concepts of Society that transcend the individual. Moreover the British and American traditions are both built on a minimalist conception of the State. In political philosophy and political theory this is bolstered with theories of representation, and of the division and limitation of powers, that implicitly define the state in instrumental terms and mostly as a necessary evil. In this tradition 'freedom' usually means *freedom from* all interference with the pursuit of individual liberty, freedom and individual happiness.

By contrast, in the German tradition since Kant, and more especially since Hegel, Society is more naturally conceived as a collective embodiment of knowledge, of reason, and of the identity of a people. Social institutions are more readily understood as the achievements of a collective 'will and consciousness'. Although Society and State are very strongly differentiated one from the other, the German tradition prefers to stress the positive and rational potentialities of both. In different ways each is seen as a medium through which individuals may rationally transcend the arbitrary limitations of individual and private life and together realize their larger purposes. Positive (and negative) notions of *the rationalization of society* have their roots in these aspects of the German tradition.

NOTES

[1] Jürgen Habermas, 'The German Idealism of the Jewish Philosophers' in *Philosophical-Political Profiles*, Cambridge, MA, 1983, as quoted by R. Berstain (ed.), *Habermas and Modernity*, p. 2.

[2] I am borrowing Bernstein's words. See note [1].

[3] The Dialectics of Rationalisation: An Interview with Jürgen Habermas, Axel Honneth *et al.*, *Telos*, **49** (Fall), 1981, p. 7.

[4] Jürgen Habermas, 'A Philosophico-Political Profile', *New Left Review*, **151**, pp. 75–105, 1985.

[5] Since Habermas rejects the Hegelian ontology of Reason (with a capital 'R') I shall follow the practice of most of Habermas's English translators and, in order to avoid confusion, use a lower case 'r' even when the term is employed in a generic sense. Sometimes, where the context allows, I shall use 'reason' interchangeably with 'rationality'.

1

Foundations

FROM THE PHILOSOPHICAL FOUNDATIONS ...

Jürgen Habermas's first major work is aptly titled *Knowledge and Human Interests* [1] (KHI). It is here that Habermas establishes the philosophical foundations for the stream of social-theoretical and sociological studies that have followed in the twenty years since the design of KHI was first announced in Habermas's inaugural lecture at Frankfurt in June of 1965. Although Habermas has had second thoughts about some aspects of KHI he still holds fast to its central convictions. It is still the best point of entry to his work.

At the very beginning of KHI, Habermas invites us to 'reconstruct' all the most essential philosophical discussions of our modern period as 'a judicial hearing' aimed at deciding the single question of 'how is reliable knowledge possible?'. And so the book is announced for what it is, namely, a comprehensive study of epistemology which, as Habermas tells us, was conceived as a 'systematic history of ideas with a practical intention' — a very unfamiliar notion indeed for anyone outside the German tradition.

Yet the unusual image of a 'judicial hearing' is a sure pointer to the heart of the whole project and to its philosophical ancestry. Immanuel Kant, the father of the German Enlightenment, and of the intellectual tradition which Habermas inherits, introduces the *Critique of Pure Reason* with the following image [2]:

> Reason ... must approach nature in order to be taught by it: but not in the character of a pupil who agrees to everything the master likes, but as an appointed judge who compels the witnesses to answer questions he himself proposes.

How is reliable knowledge possible? Although the detail and method of Habermas's arguments are both difficult and foreign for the British reader the answer is, in a general way, very clear, and very Kantian in character.

Reliable knowledge is only possible when science assumes its proper, subordinate place as *one* of the accomplishments of reason [3]. KHI is a history of ideas with a 'practical intention' inasmuch as its aim, its practical intention, is to rescue the rationalist heritage and to retrace the steps which reason has taken to its prison in the cellars of modern science.

Habermas is more than willing to honour the achievements of science. He is *for* science and (like Kant 200 years before him) he will defend it against dogmatic metaphysics and, in our own time, against the romantic views of Nature and against the attacks of conservatives who want to oppose it with blind traditions. His purpose is to insist that science should be done better, in a more philosophically knowing way, and so with *tougher* epistemological standards! The focus of his criticisms — of modernity, and of the modern epistemology that rules over just about every branch of modern learning from natural science to the humanities — is the *relationship* between science and philosophy. *Knowledge and Human Interests* is a critique of modern positivism. It seeks to show how positivism has mutilated our reason and swallowed it whole into a limited theory and practice of science. The 'practical intent' of this history of ideas is to trace the gradual establishment of positivism and thus exhume the larger concept of reason that it has sought to bury. It is therefore not an attack on science but an attack rather upon an arrogant and mistaken self-understanding of science that reduces all knowledge to a belief in itself. He calls this 'scientism' and it means [4],

> science's belief in itself: that is, the conviction that we can no longer understand science as *one* form of possible knowledge, but rather must identify knowledge with science.

Scientism is also the 'basic orientation prevailing in analytic philosophy, until recently the most ... influential philosophy of our time'. The claim which he seeks to vindicate in three hundred pages of brilliant but difficult argument is that [5]

> science can only be comprehended epistemologically, which means as one category of possible knowlege, as long as knowledge is not equated with ... scientistic self-understanding of the actual business of [scientific] research.

He wants to rescue the more 'comprehensive rationality of reason that has not yet shrunk to a set of methodological principles'. Accordingly, the task of KHI is to outline, and to justify, a more comprehensive epistemology (with tougher standards) that can rehabilitate the claims of reason in human affairs. In terms of the Kantian metaphor he must restore the authority of the 'judge'. This he does by means of 'critical reconstructions' first of Kant and then of Hegel, Comte and Mach, Pierce, Dilthey, Freud and Nietzsche among others. All these criticisms are aimed at identifying the errors which would cumulatively lead to the bankruptcy of reason in modern philosophy and science. Our problem is that these discussions mostly presuppose an intimate knowledge of the classical figures whom Habermas addresses almost as partners in a dialogue. Yet, as we shall see, the basic outlines of the epistemology that Habermas hopes to vindicate can be summarized without too much difficulty.

This will be easier if we have in mind the following elementary schema.

Subject	Action	Object
I	think	it
I	know	it
I	perceive	it
I	understand	it
I	interpret	it
I	posit	it

(left bracket label: the inter-subjective world) (right bracket label: the objective world)

At the centre of the schema are some transitive verbs refering to knowledge and belief. The first, obvious but nonetheless basic, point is, of course, that every act of knowing, perceiving, etc. is a human *action* that must, accordingly, have a subject and an object. Even with these elementary terms we can begin to grasp the common motif of Habermas's careful arguments against the 'objectivistic illusion of unreflecting science', that is, of modern positivism. Every undergraduate with a unit of behavioural psychology in his or her academic record will have had some experience of the most vulgar example of what Habermas means. In this, as in every other field of positivistic science, we are asked to approach the object world as a disaggregated jumble of discrete objects of perception, as a jumble of 'its'. We are set the task of uncovering the regularities in the behaviour of these atoms of substance by means of an experimental method. The criterion of success lies in the predictive power of the uncovered 'laws' that must produce replicable results. This means results that are *independent* of the author, the inventor, in short of the *thinking subject* who in the first place conceived the problem, the method and the experiment and who thereby created the knowledge. One half of the underlying assumption is that knowledge is always reducible to the totality of discovered properties of the object world. The other half is that the *subject* — the actor, the creator, the knower, the inventor, the scientist — is at worst a pollutant in his own purely objective world, or at best, a ghost in the machine of science and something that must be methodologically controlled and, so far as is possible, eliminated. In a nutshell these are the assumptions of a positivist science that occasioned such hot debate over the nature and theory of science in the 1970s. They still underlie public perceptions of science and the mundane practice of science in every field at the botton of the pyramid of modern science. Habermas joined those debates [6] with the aim of challenging, at the apex of the pyramid, the *source* of these epistemological assumptions in the orthodox empiricism that still dominates most theories of science.

Let us return for a moment to this simple image of subject–knower––object. Habermas has three aims:

(1) The first is to explain, in a similar way to Kant 200 years before him, that knowledge is necessarily defined *both* by the objects of experience *and* by *a priori* categories and concepts *that the knowing subject brings to every act of thought and perception*. Even 'space' and 'time', the basic notions of such rigorous sciences as physics, are not supplied by experience alone. Indeed, as Kant argued in the *Critique of Pure Reason*, they make no sense without concepts, ideas, that are given *a priori*, independently of all experience. Ideas and concepts are not simply, as classical empiricism since Hume would have it, merely 'weak sense impressions'. They are *not* derivations of experience but *constituents* of it: the essential constituents of logic are *not* copied or taken from the object world; instead they are given in the categories and forms that the subject brings to the act of perception. The validity of scientific knowledge, of hermeneutic understanding, and of mundane knowledge always depends as much on its 'subjective', and inter-subjective, constituents as it does on any methodologically verifiable observation and experience of the object-world. So, we can see that Habermas's aim is to 'put reason and rationality back into the knowing subject'. It would be entirely misleading to cast Habermas as a neo-classical idealist [7] — although this is just what some of his critics, orthodox marxists [8] and others, have tried to do. Habermas explicitly rejects the idealist epistemology of innate ideas! However, it is clear that his whole work hangs on the solidity of an epistemology in which the validation of knowledge and understanding is returned to the knowing and reasoning subject.

(2) His second aim is to show that the knowing subject is also *social* and, as we shall see later, dynamic as well. Here there is a sharp break with Kant and with the classical philosophical tradition in which epistemological questions are treated as the concern of a solitary individual confronted with the puzzle of the universe. The modernization of the

Kantian legacy requires, with Hegel and Marx, a full recognition of the fact that knowledge and understanding are socially coordinated and at every moment conditioned and mediated by our historical experience. Kant's philosophical arguments are cast, as were those of classical Greek philosophy, into a timeless world outside history and, to some extent, beyond social experience as well. One of the aims of KHI is to secure the foundations of sociology and to show that there is no knower without culture, and that *all knowledge is mediated by social experience*. The knower is, of course, not surrendered to the empiricist prejudice that the subject is, once more, a mere reflex of the object world, or that ideas are, again, just weak sense impressions, the imprints of the object world that form it only 'from the outside in'. On the contrary, the subject still brings its own categories and 'faculties of reason' to the constitution of the object and thus to the formative moment of knowledge. As we shall see later the distinctive feature of Habermas's work is that processes of knowing and understanding are grounded, not in philosophically dubious notions of a transcendental ego, but rather in the patterns of ordinary language usage that we share in everyday communicative interaction.

(3) The third aim is to establish the validity of reflection. Every theory of knowledge must deal with the problem — potentially an infinitely regressive problem — of how it is that we find the knowledge with which to correct the knowledge that is now in doubt, and so on *ad infinitum*. Habermas's aim is to show that the power of reason is grounded in the process of reflection, and from this perspective, to counter the usual claim of traditional (British) empiricism that reflection conceived in this German way is just illusory introspection and, of course, that the only remedy for such defective knowledge is to be found in an ever more exact understanding of external Nature [9].

Habermas has no wish to protect bad science and he certainly wants imperfect knowledge to be corrected with better scientific observation where that is appropriate. His larger argument is that the defects of imperfect knowledge — and this is simply another term for *irrationality* — originate in the 'cognitive attitude' of scientistic (positivist) science. Empiricism is a fundamentally misconceived attitude that has warped the logic of science in such a way that the scientific community cannot [10],

> perceive itself as the *subject of reflection*. By their scientific orientation, its members are obliged to objectivate themselves. Unable to meet the demand for self-reflection without simultaneous abandonment of their theory, they reject that demand by conceiving a programme of science theory which would make all demands of self-reflection *immaterial*.

In other words, the terms that we bring from within ourselves to the process of enquiry — in any and every domain, including science — are amenable to a reflection that is *rational* for the very reason that it carries the potential for a more inclusive conceptualization that is better attuned to the common interest of the human condition.

These three aims are worked out in Habermas's 'theory of knowledge–constitutive interests' that he first stated in the inaugural Frankfurt lecture in 1965 [11]. The theory systematically explains the threefold structure of his epistemology. It is central to all his work and rather easier to grasp than the daunting jargon might otherwise suggest.

Some of the essential elements have already been suggested. In thought and action we simultaneously *both* create *and* discover the world; and knowledge crystallizes in this generative relation of the subject to the world. Every 'speaking and acting subject' constitutes knowledge, however idiosyncratically and variably, in the light of three universally given 'knowledge-constitutive interests', or 'cognitive interests', that are given *a priori* in our relation to the world [12] (see Table 1).

Table 1

Cognitive interest	Type of science	Knowledge	Social medium	Domain
Technical control	Natural sciences (empirical/ analytic)	Technical or instrumental knowledge	Work	Nature
Practical	Historical/ hermeneutic (*Geisteswissen-schaften*)	Practical	Language	Society
Emancipation autonomy	Critical sciences	Emancipation	Authority	

In the case of the natural or 'empirical-analytic' sciences (*Naturwissenschaften*), it is our universal interest in the technical control of nature that constitutes 'the meaning of possible statements and establishes rules *both* for the construction of theories *and* for their critical testing' [13]. This is, as we have seen, the basis of Habermas's critical rejection of classical empiricism. There is no defensible basis for an ontology of an independently existing world of things 'out there' that constitute knowledge objectivistically, 'from the outside in' and according to a correspondence theory of truth — a mistaken assumption that each atom of knowledge must correspond with an atom of independently existing substance. This is not a denial of objective reality. The point is rather that what we know about nature is always defined by the cognitive attitude which informs our scientific enquiry. Habermas insists that, in this domain, our attitude is fundamentally instrumental. Nature is conceived, even in the theoretical and 'pure' sciences, in terms of our interest in controlling it. That, at any rate, is the *telos*, the implicit objective, of all scientific enquiry.

As a species we have a second universal interest, namely in mutual understanding in the everyday conduct of life. To understand what this means we must again overcome the prejudices of parts of the liberal British philosophical tradition in which other individual human beings are set on a par with objects in nature and apprehended with the same objectivist epistemology by a supposedly self-sufficient individual knower. Habermas insists that the 'objectivity of experience consists precisely in its being intersubjectively shared' [14]. In everyday social interaction, as in all studies of society, literature, art and history, our understanding presupposes a 'pre-understanding' [15] of the other speaking and acting subjects whose meanings we seek to interpret. The proof of this is that socialization is a universal precondition for individual identity: the specific contents of my subjective world may be very different to those of your inner world but, like it or not, I can have no coherent identity unless I can enter your experience in a way that allows me to understand what you *mean*. The same is true for you and so we share with all other human beings, in every place and time, a universal interest in the mutual self-understanding that underpins all social action. Habermas calls this the 'practical' interest that constitutes knowledge in the 'historical-hermeneutic' sciences — the clumsy term that, in the absence of a notion of '*Geist*' (collective mind? spirit? consciousness?), a term we must use to translate '*Geisteswissenschaften*', a term that is so naturally paired in the German tradition with '*Naturwissenschaften*'.

There is a third knowledge-constitutive interest that is, as we shall see in a moment, even more firmly tied to the German Hegelian and Marxist tradition. In everyday experience there is a part of us that tries, however, unsuccessfully, to differentiate between power and truth, or in other words to penetrate illusions that veil arbitrary power in society. In a related way the 'critical sciences' presuppose a common interest in adult autonomy, in 'truth, freedom and justice', and in emancipation from ideologically frozen representations of all politically constituted order. This 'emancipatory' interest is the vehicle through which 'emancipatory knowledge' (that means reason and fully rational knowledge) is reinstated in the other two domains. It will be the task of critical reflection to grub out the positivist root (in realist, materialist, and other modern empiricist philosophies of science) and thus to once again put science back into the *service* of human rationality. It will have the same task in history and literary studies where other strands of the same epistemology have produced the same kind of irrational reductionism: whereas the German historicist tradition is Habermas's prime example of disguised positivism in humanistic studies, in our culture a better example may well be the British Leavisite tradition of literary criticism in which texts are treated as pure objects.

In the face of much criticism Habermas has accepted that his cherished notion of emancipatory reflection joins two ideas that pull in rather different directions. On the one hand, reflection means reason's reflections upon its own principles and categories in the usual Kantian sense of 'critique', and, on the other hand, Habermas loads in the second and logically distinct idea of reflection as a form of self-formation (*Bildung*) which emancipates as it dissolves the constraining spell of false beliefs — this is the other strand that is carried from Hegel into the young Marx (and with which I shall deal in the last section of this chapter). In his own scrupulously honest way Habermas admits these difficulties and deals with them in the course of his later work. For the moment we need only emphasize again the centrality of this threefold system of categories which recurs again and again in all his philosophical and sociological texts.

Knowledge and Human Interests is an attempt to set the foundations for a critical theory that would stand 'between philosophy and science'. The very need for such an extensive reworking of epistemological foundations tells us something about the relationship between philosophy and power. Habermas's view of ideology, in this formative stage of his work, has nothing in common with the hopelessly shallow liberal notion in which ideology is seen merely as bad science or as the corrupted exaggeration of political rhetoric. If ideology had no greater penetration than this, such a project as Habermas has undertaken would be a preposterously extravagant response. New epistemological groundings are necessary because ideology — by this we mean all ideas that either hide or legitimate arbitrary power — *reaches back into the very constitution of knowledge in society*. It points to a need for an equally fundamental and careful critical re-appraisal of sociological perspectives.

TO THE SOCIOLOGICAL RECONSTRUCTIONS ...

Habermas has used the classical foundation tests of sociology as the building blocks for his own comprehensive social theory. He takes the work of each of the 'fathers' which he then reconstructs to extract the core that is still of decisive contemporary importance. He explains that: reconstruction signifies taking a theory apart and putting it back together again in a new form in order to attain more fully the goal it has set for itself [16]. His reconstructions of Durkheim, Mead and Parsons are all very important constitutents of his theory — yet, since Habermas is so steeped in his own German tradition, it is his reconstructions of Weber and Marx which should have priority in these few illustrative remarks that follow.

Marx

In the West today there is an active competition between three different interpretations of Marx. There is the anti-philosophical, orthodox marxism of important and often British figures such as Mandel, Anderson, Braverman, Baran and Sweezy,and Bottomore, which still accepts historical materialism at something close to face value. Secondly, there is the French neo-orthodox or 'scientific' marxism that we associate first with Althusser and Poulantzas and now with the post-structuralist tradition into which it has largely dissolved. A third variant is sometimes called 'humanistic' inasmuch as it reads Marx more philosophically, in his own German tradition, through the residues of Hegel, and in a way that gives far greater importance to the role of ideas in history.

Habermas's reconstructions of Marx clearly belong to the third stream. In his eyes the other two variants are seen as 'scientistic' because they rely on a positivist history or a positivist economic theory, or both. Habermas's marxism is cautious, tentative, and self-critical. He is far removed from workers and working classes, but for all this is still certainly a man driven, above all, by an intelluctual anticipation of a world in which production, labour, and social organization are geared *rationally to human needs* rather than, as now in the West, irrationally to capital accumulation (profit).

As we shall see later in considering his political sociology Habermas's reconstruction retains a view of market relations between wage-labour and capital as the main source of exploitation and power in capitalist society. The political sociology is aimed, as any attempt to convincingly relate Marx to modern-day 'late' or 'advanced' capitalist society must be, at the need to understand the role of the State and of ideology in mass democracies. Here we should note only that, in so far as it addresses the contemporary realities of advanced capitalism, the reconstruction abandons the two foundations of orthodox and scientific marxism, namely the labour theory of value and with it the notion of class.

The positive thrust of Habermas's reconstruction takes a direction that is adumbrated as follows [17]:

Marx wanted to capture the embodiments of unreason. In the same sense, we are also concerned today with the analysis of power constellations that supress an intention intrinsic to the ... claim to reason announced in the teleological and inter-subjective structures of social reproduction themselves. Again and again this claim is silenced; and yet in fantasies and deeds it develops a stubbornly transcending power, because it is renewed with each act of unconstrained understanding, with each moment of living together in solidarity, of successful individuation, and of saving emancipation .... Like Marx's, my theoretical approach is guided by the intention of recovering a potential for reason encapsulated in the very forms of social reproduction.

Here Habermas points to the two basic elements in his reconstruction of Marx's underdeveloped theory of social evolution that we call 'historical materialism'.

In the first place, as we shall see later in some greater detail, he wants to put those 'inter-subjective and teleological structures of social reproduction' in a long-historical perspective that will correct the economic reductionism of Marx's later work. The history of human society cannot be framed in a narrow way as an economically determined progress through five different modes of production: of hunter/gatherer (= primitive communism), the asiatic mode of production, the feudal, the capitalist and then the communist or 'post-capitalist'. This is an inadequate grounding for Marx's own critical social theory because it projects explanation 'backwards' from out of the very thing — capitalism — which we seek to understand, not in a mistaken way as an 'ontological constant', but instead as a particular and historically transient phenomenon. All this reworking is necessary to give some defensible substance to Marx's social anthropology and to his underdeveloped theory of social evolution. But the price we have to pay 'to make Marx stick' at this deeper level is the abandonment of the 'paradigm of production'.

The second and related purpose is, as Agnes Heller [18] explains so clearly, to redefine what classical marxism reads as the 'independent variable' of social evolution, namely the forces of production, i.e. technology and technologically useful instrumental knowledge. Here Habermas's reconstruction of Marx is an attempt to establish the crucial importance of knowledge in history and to incorporate into the marxist heritage a theory of culture that is not positivistically reduced to economic processes. Even in the early writings Habermas insisted that labour was an 'epistemological category', the aspect under which Nature becomes known to us, and not solely an economic category. From that epistemological viewpoint labour means 'instrumental' and technological knowledge that is socially coordinated and so rooted in culture and bound up with forms of symbolic interaction that characterize each stage of social evolution. Insofar as we judge him to have succeeded, he purges orthodox marxism of its naive nineteenth-century belief in the sheer force of material 'toolpower' *per se* as an independent force for human development. It is replaced with a demystified recognition of what the forces of production really are, namely '*an endogenous growth of human knowledge*'. Accordingly, we must reconstruct social evolution as a progress that depends on expanded possibilities for *learning* and so for the creation of culture with an emancipatory potential: as the progressive institutionalization of the claims of reason against arbitrary power.

Weber

The orientation of Habermas's social theory is fundamentally Weberian inasmuch as he wants to analyse culture, knowledge and reason as forms of what Weber, in his famous definitions of sociology [19], called 'meaningful social action'. For Habermas, as we have seen, culture is action because it is always something that *subjects do*, whether in thought or deed. It is no accident that the first volume of Habermas's latest and most important work should be titled 'Reason and the Rationalisation of Society' [20]. It takes up Max Weber's central preoccupation with the process of rationalization and 'disenchantment'. Furthermore, it clearly has its taproot in Weber's explanations of the relation between culture and economy in the *Protestant Ethic and the Spirit of Capitalism* [21] — or, in Weber's vocabulary, between 'ideal' and 'material' interests.

It may be useful to think of Habermas's reconstructions of Weber as a three-sided pyramid (see Fig. 1) whose base is built on reworked connections between three fundamentally Weberian notions of (a) social action, (b) rationality, and (c) rationalization.

The reconstruction sets out to systematically rework the confused and unsystematic relation between action and rationality in Weber. The ultimate purpose is to secure the three foundations so that they will support and vindicate, at the apex of the pyramid, Habermas's own central notion of 'communicative rationality'. All of the reconstructions in *Reason and the Rationalisation of Society* aim at providing a defensible basis for this central idea — so that we can use it 'without blushing' to address the problems of late capitalist society in our own age. With over four hundred pages of difficult but often brilliant argument Habermas sets out to show that 'communicative rationality' is the hidden normative standard behind Weber's outwardly restrained but nonetheless passionate and despairing denunciation of the 'iron cage' of modern capitalism.

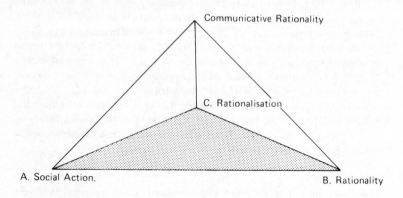

Fig. 1 — The 'reconstruction' of Weber.

One side of the base (A–B) involves a reworking of Weber's inappropriate assimilation of social action with the four gradations of rationality which Habermas represents with Schluchter [22] as shown in Table 2. The

Table 2

Types of action in descending order of rationality	Subjective meaning covers the following:			
	means	ends	values	consequences
Purposive-rationality (*Zweckrationalität*)	+	+	+	+
Value-rationality (*Wertrationalität*)	+	+	+	–
Affectual	+	+	–	–
Traditional	+	–	–	–

aim of the reconstruction is to counter what we only glimpse here as Weber's implicit tendency to give a pseudo-normative force to 'purposive' or 'instrumental' rationality by treating all other forms as derivations and degradations of it. With a question that expresses both the intention and the pain of his first attempts to recast these categories Haberman asks, why is it that 'only purposive-rational action and not value-rational action is sup-posed to have *structure-forming effects*' [23]. He wants to oppose Weber's outward ethical scepticism [24] and, within a modification of Weber's own framework, to capture, systematically, the tremendous force of Weber's ethical vision that gathers about such confused notions as 'practical rationa-lity', 'substantive rationality' and 'an ethic of responsibility'. Weber's concept of 'meaningful social action' is reconstrued, and action and rationality are re-joined, in a theory of 'speech acts' that is sometimes referred to as 'the linguistic turn' of Habermas's later work. However, the aim is clear enough. Habermas wants to show that the validity claims of both practical/ethical statements arise in ordinary social *inter-action* together with claims about the truth of this or that state of affairs, and that *both* are equally capable of 'rational redemption'.

With respect to the second baseline (B–C) and the connection between rationality and the world/historical process of rationalization first enun-ciated in the 'Protestant Ethic', Habermas will again try, so to speak, to make Weber true to his own project. This involves taking sides against the usual British and American *empiricist* interpretations of Weber in order to rehabilitate him within his own German — Kantian, Hegelian, and Marxist — tradition [25]. This gives greater prominence to rationalization as a world-historical process construed as a *cultural* process that is grounded in a progress of ideas with its own partially independent dynamic, its own internal 'logic', and with its own potential for rationalization in the positive, emancipatory sense. Two bold reformulations of Weber's whole work are designed to secure this goal. In the first place Habermas argues, I think very plausibly, that it is Weber's sociology of religion (and with it of ideas and culture) that stands at the heart of his work [26] and holds the key to his understanding of the rationalization process. Of course this happens to be just the part of Weber that best thwarts the positivistic reduction of culture to science, because here, in the sociology of religion, the progress of ideas *leads* the growth of science. Habermas's strategy is therefore to assimilate large tracts of Weber that *are* more positivistically inclined — especially the sociology of law and Weber's view of politics and the State — with a sociology of religion that is in keeping with Weber's own, Kantian and German Enlightenment, heritage. Secondly, Habermas must make Weber's view of the rationalization process compatible with a cognitivist theory of ethics, that is to say with a theory of ethics that recognizes the incipiently *rational form* of ethical world views in human history and is therefore strong enough to defeat the empiricist reduction of ethics to mere habits, conventions and passions, or arbitrary traditions.

The third baseline (A–C) that connects social action with rationaliza-tion is another face of Habermas's theory of social evolution. His aim is, as we shall see, to uncover the unfolding potential for genuine rationalization that is released and secured in each of the stages of social evolution. In other words the task of the reconstruction here is to save Weber, the 'despairing liberal' [27], from his own entirely pessimistic prognosis of the rationalization of late capitalism (the inexorable process that produces only 'sensualists without spirit, specialists without heart', etc. and locks us all into the 'iron cage'). From his consideration of the two theses, of 'rationalization as the loss of meaning' and 'rationalization as the loss of freedom' [28], Habermas extracts a third *positive* thesis that we may roughly paraphrase as 'rationalization as the expanded possibility for collective learning and as the (gradual) institutionalization of reason in Society'. It is along these lines that Weber's theory of rationalization as a world-historical process is assimilated with the reconstruction of Marx's historical materialism.

AND THE RECONSTITUTION OF CRITICAL THEORY

The Frankfurt School, as it came to be known, was the first institute for marxist studies in the Western world. It was set up at Frankfurt University in 1923 with money provided by Felix Weil, a wealthy industrialist. From 1930 under the directorship of Max Horkheimer, significantly himself a philosopher by training, the leading members of the Institute, among them Adorno, Marcuse, Pollock, Benjamin (an associate member), Lowenthal and Fromm, developed a distinctive identity as the new voices of this humanistic marxism cum critical theory. All of them were Jews, and those who fled the holocaust rejoined the Institute for Social Research in its new home at the centre of the capitalist world in New York City at Columbia University from 1934. Research in the important post-war period covered several themes including the development of critical theory, the nature and emergence of fascism, authority and the family, and art and popular culture.

Although Habermas was scarcely born in the early Horkheimer years when the School was attracting its most prominent members, he did know most of those who survived the war and was considerably influenced by Horkheimer, Marcuse, and Adorno, in particular. More importantly, he was, in his own formative period, himself steeped in the same scholarly tradition that had shaped them. The most important modern influence — certainly for Habermas in his own early period — is the Hegelianized marxism of Lukács (and Korsch) and of the left 'philosophy of consciousness' (a very Hegelian idea). Lukács is so important because he incorporates a new and potent element, namely Max Weber, into this Hegelianized reading of Marx. For the Frankfurt School, it is, on the one hand, the Hegelian strand that intellectually redeems the marxist tradition, in theory, from what was, in practice, the horrific failure of Stalinism and Soviet bureaucratic state socialism. Through Lukács, critical theory restores to marxism a strongly philosophical image of the history-making subject as the bearer of redemptive reason in society. On the other hand, the equally important Weberian strand provides the key to the institutional character of Western capitalism and, more particularly, of the fascist State and of Stalin's repressive bureaucracy. Through Lukács the Frankfurt School joins Weber's analysis of rationalization and disenchantment — of 'rationalization as the loss of freedom' and of 'rationalization as the loss of meaning' — with Marx's analysis of the commodity form. In this way the Frankfurt School brings Marx and Weber together in a many-sided study of *reification*, of 'false consciousness' and of ideology in late capitalism — in its art (Benjamin), in its popular culture (Adorno), in economics (Pollock), in psychology and the family (Adorno, Fromm) and in science (Marcuse).

It is true that Habermas is 'the heir to the Frankfurt School' and yet this has become something of a cliché, and a misleading one at that. Habermas does not have much in common with the early work of the Frankfurt School before the Second World War. Despite its many innovations, that work was still firmly anchored in a marxian philosophical anthropology of labour. But he does have a much closer affinity with the critical theory that emerges from the *Dialectic of Enlightenment* because it has a larger appreciation of the partially independent role that ideas, symbolic representation, 'mimesis', and even language have in the struggle for emancipation. However, the insights are still too vague. Habermas is therefore more concerned with his own systematic and rigorous reconstructions of his classical figures — Kant, Hegel, Marx, Dilthey, Weber, Freud, Durkheim, Parsons, Mead and others — than he is with the work of his forebears in the Frankfurt School to whom he gives respectful deference and not very much attention. His aim is not to qualify or even to build upon the work of Horkheimer, Adorno, and Marcuse, but rather to reconstitute the whole 'paradigm' of critical theory.

One basic insight that guides the reconstruction is Habermas's recognition of the intellectual costs of continued fidelity to Hegel. In the German social philosophical tradition of Hegel it has been natural to view history as a rational process that proceeds *dialectically*. The society that exists presently (society 1) calls up a negating image of the better alternative (society 2) and, if the contradiction is sufficiently fundamental, there is the possibility of a synthesis (society 3), in which humankind advances one step further in a history that leads to the rational self-fulfilment of the species.

This is an underlying motif in the 'philosophical' or 'humanistic' marxism of the early Lukács, and it is an important constituent in the work of Marcuse and Adorno and, in varying degrees, of the other members of the Frankfurt School. However, Habermas believes that the costs 'of concepts of totality, of truth, and of theory derived from Hegel' now represent, 'too heavy a mortgage on a theory of society which should satisfy empirical claims' [29]. Habermas's views on this matter are instructive because they clarify his criticisms of his forebears and, at the same time, indicate what is different and important in his own work. There are three important points [30].

(1) In a criticism that is perhaps principally aimed at Adorno, Habermas ventures that the Hegelian 'paradigm' is unworkable because as scholars, 'we cannot live with the paradoxes of negative dialectics' — of a totalizing Reason that is supposed to be positive in the very 'moment' of negation. The paradigm simply does not work: it is too negative in the plain garden sense of the term and this partly accounts for critical theory's near total *lack of any clear (positive) normative standards* for its critique. This is why Habermas has, in the ten and more years since his first formulations of the 'ideal-speech situation', gone to such pains to spell out the details of his own normative standard in the notion of 'communicative rationality'.

(2) A second problem is that the Hegelian concept of truth — originally of the Absolute Idea actualizing itself in a progress of critical self-reflection — fails hopelessly when, at ground level, it comes up against modern empirical social and natural science. The response of some members of the Frankfurt School was to protect the Hegelian idea of truth only in the realm of intention and, at the same time, either to give it up in closer empirically oriented arguments, or, worse, as in Marcuse's case to attack the very form of modern science as a positivistic reification. This, Habermas will not accept: as we have seen, he instead develops a detailed neo-Kantian epistemology that will allow him to meet and to differentiate between the respective truth claims of different spheres of science and scholarship — of science, ethics, and aesthetics.

(3) Another problem is that, once joined with the marxist critique, the Hegelian paradigm leads to a wholly negative dismissal of the achievements of bourgeois institutions. All the historical achievements they embody — the bourgeois state, civil law, the 'rights' of the individual, and the differentiation and partial autonomy of religion, politics, science and art — are denied in the intellectual anticipation of their dialectical cum revolutionary negation. There is a fundamental flaw in

the utopian critique (Lukács and others) that is so diffuse that it cannot distinguish the traces of reason amid the irrationalities of bourgeois society. Habermas insists that a well-grounded social theory, one that reconstructs Marx's analysis of captialism more rigorously and in a longer historical perspective, should instead offer a more precise view of the rationalization process. The more adequate social theory will overcome the problems of its Hegelian and philosophical origins, and support specific, and focused, analyses of the concrete 'sites' of irrationality, such as environmental degradation, unemployment, militarism, the manipulation of public opinon by the mass media and bureaucratization.

In short, critical theory requires a thorough reconstitution that will save it from 'its dead ends in the philosophy of consciousness'. This amounts to a whole paradigmatic change that lifts the central problem — of negative versus positive rationalization — out of its left-Hegelian philosophical paradigm and re-situates it in a more classically sociological context. The reconstituted social theory is still aimed at essentially the same fundamental problem of negative rationalization — a problem that we can inelegantly summarize with the following formula: Rationalization as the loss of meaning + Rationalization as the loss of freedom = Reification = the increasing penetration of exchange values and power into society, culture, and the lifeworld (*Lebenswelt*). Yet the reconstitution is no less fundamental because it is concerned, above all, with groundings and with the articulation of its own normative standards.

The reconstituted social theory is supposed to provide a thoroughly grounded explanation of how society has assumed its present form and character. More specifically, Habermas's theory offers a step-by-step reconstruction of the rationalization process, and of its course of development charted against its own normative standard of 'communicative rationality'. The origins, correlates, and expressions of this standard are explored in detailed studies of developmental psychology, social evolution, the history of ideas, the political constitution of modern society and in the problems of modernity. In his criticisms of the older critical theory Habermas announces the extraordinarily demanding criteria on which he is prepared to be judged. The theory is not offered as a drug for perpetual adolescents who yearn for intimations of utopia, but rather as a hard body of theory that can enter the university and rationally ground successful challenges to the stubbornly resistant false science embedded in the research agendas and curricula of modern economics, philosophy, history, sociology, psychology, anthropology, politics, the humanities, and all the multi-disciplinary and applied fields such as education, urban planning, etc. A tall order indeed! It is to the broad lines of this mighty project that we turn in the following chapters.

NOTES

[1] Jürgen Habermas, *Knowledge and Human Interests,* trans. Jeremy Shapiro, Heinemann, London, 1972. Hereafter KHI.

[2] Immanuel Kant, *The Critique of Pure Reason*, trans. F. Max Muller, Doubleday Anchor, New York, 1966, p. 16.

[3] See the note about Reason with a capital 'R' in note [5] of the preceding introduction.

[4] KHI, p. 4.

[5] KHI, p, 4.

[6] T. Adorno *et al.* (eds), *The Positivist Debate in German Sociology*, Heinemann, London, 1982.

[7] This is how he is seen by Kolakowski, *Main currents of Marxism*, Oxford University Press, Vol. III, pp. 393–394.

[8] For example see in this same series the unsympathetic criticisms of Tom Bottomore in *The Frankfurt School* (Key Sociologists series), Ellis Horwood, Chichester; Tavistock Publications, London, 1984.

[9] Because, as David Hume would have it, 'all our ideas, or *weak* perceptions, are derived from our impression or *strong* perceptions and ... [that] ... accordingly, whenever any idea is ambiguous he ... [the philosopher] ... has always recourse to the impression which must render it clear and precise', David Hume, *On Human Nature and the Understanding*, ed. A. Flew, Collier Macmillan, 1962, p. 291.

[10] 'A Postscript to Knowledge and Human Interests', *Philosophy of the Social Sciences,* 3, 1973, 157–189, see p. 161. This postscript is included in most later editions of the book KHI but it is not to be confused with the *appendix* containing the 1965 inaugural Frankfurt lecture.

[11] Available as the appendix (not to be confused with the postscript) to KHI and, in journal form, as 'Knowledge and Interest', *Inquiry*, 9, 4, 1966.

[12] The diagram is adapted from one provided with many useful explanations of this early formulation by Guttorm Floistad, 'Social Concepts of Action: Notes on Habermas' Proposal for a Social Theory of Action', *Inquiry*, 13, 1970, pp. 175–199.

[13] KHI, p. 308.

[14] A Postscript to KHI, p. 168.

[15] This notion that is so essential to the modern German tradition of the *Geisteswissenschaften* comes from Heidegger.

[16] Habermas, *Communication and the Evolution of Society*, trans. T. McCarthy, Beacon Press, Boston, 1979, p. 95.

[17] In Habermas, 'A Reply to my Critics', which appears as the last chapter in *Habermas: Critical Debates*, John Thompson and David Held (eds), Macmillan, London, 1982, p. 221.

[18] Agnes Heller in 'Habermas and Marxism', Chapter 1, of *Habermas: Critical Debates* (see note [17]).

[19] Max Weber, *Economy and Society*, Vol. 1, G. Roth and C. Wittich (eds) University of California Press, pp. 4–24.

[20] *Theorie des kommunikativen Handelns*, Band 1, *Handlungsrationalität und gesellschaftliche Rationalisierung*, Vol. 1, trans. Tom McCarthy, *Reason and the Rationalisation of Society*, Heinemann, London, 1981. Hereafter RRS. McCarthy is at present translating the second volume that is to appear in 1987.

[21] See especially the last ten pages of PESC and also the 'Die Wirtschaftsethik der Weltreligionen', *Gesammelte Aufsätze zur Religionssoziologie*, translated as 'The Social Psychology of World Religions' and available in Gerth and Mills collection, *From Max Weber*, pp. 267–301. Habermas agrees with the important arguments of Tenbruck that these texts in Weber's sociology of religion hold the key to the whole of Weber's work. See F. H. Tenbruck, 'Das Werk Max Weber's *Kölner Zeitschrift für Soziologie und Sozialpsychologie*, 27, 1975, and, for an interpretation of the debate, S. Kalberg, 'The Discussion of Max Weber in Recent German Sociological Literature', *Sociology*, 13, 1979.

[22] Habermas uses this scheme in a first short statement 'Aspects of the Rationality of Action' in *Rationality Today*, Theodore F. Geraets (ed.), University of Ottawa Press, 1979, p. 194. He uses it again in a more extensive discussion in RRS: see esp. p. 292f. It is adapted from the important work of Wolfgang Schluchter, translated as the *Rise of Western Rationalisation*, University of California Press, 1981.

[23] Habermas in *Rationality Today*, p. 191 (see note [22]).

[24] Most evident in his essays on the methodology of the social sciences that were so misleadingly affirmed, in the empiricist reading of Weber, as the key to his view not only of methodology but also, most inappropriately, of society itself.

[25] And so with the reading of Weber that is to be found in Löwith, Schluchter, Tenbruck, and to some extent Mommsen.

[26] This is the view argued by F. Tenbruck. 'The Problem of Thematic Unity in the Work of Max Weber', *British J. of Sociology*.

[27] This is Mommsen's label.
[28] See RRS, Ch. 4.
[29] Habermas, 'A Philosophico-Political Profile', an interview, *New Left Review*, **151**, 1985, pp. 75–105, see p. 78.
[30] Habermas, 'The Dialectics of Rationalisation: an interview with Jürgen Habermas' by Alex Honneth *et al.*, *Telos*. **49**, pp. 4–31.

2

Culture, evolution, rationalization and method

> The release of a potential for reason embedded in communicative
> action is a world-historical process; in the modern period it leads
> to a rationalisation of life-worlds, to the differentiation of their
> symbolic structures, which is expressed above all in the increasing
> reflexivity of cultural traditions, in processes of individuation, in
> the generalisation of values, in the increasing prevalence of more
> abstract and more universal norms, etc. [1].

INTRODUCTION

In this chapter I want to address three topics. They were chosen because
each has an importance in its own right as a discrete aspect of Habermas's
work and, equally, because all three are basic constituents of his larger
critical social theory of our 'advanced' or 'late' capitalist society.

The first topic, namely Habermas's long-historical theory of the evolution of society, gives us a view of his social anthropology. It also provides a
clearer picture of his reconstructions of historical materialism. The second
topic is Habermas's explanation, accomplished through his reconstruction
of Weber's theory of rationalization, of the all-important transition from
'traditional' to 'modern' society, a process that begins long before the
industrial revolution and is still working itself out today. The third section
of the chapter deals briefly with some problems of method, meaning and
causation.

A moment's reflection on what was said in the preceding chapter will
prompt us to seek and to find the same underlying purposes in all three
topics. Habermas has entered these discussions — about social anthropo-

logy; the economic, social and cultural history of Europe; hermeneutics and the methodology of the social sciences — in order better to ground the several constituents of his theory of our own late capitalist society. The groundings have a great importance and, in Habermas's case, there is no choice but to accept that the keys to the rooms with the best view are kept in the basement. In each of these discussions he is, in different ways, trying to explain the progress of Reason in history (the reconstructed Hegelian thread); to trace the course of a world-historical process of rationalization (the Weberian thread) and to show how this process relates to power, economy and nature (the reconstruction of Marx's historical materialism). To achieve these aims he must, in all three discussions, succeed in persuading us that reason, rationality and truth, confront us in worldviews (*Weltanschauungen*), in culture, in history, and in the norms and values that guide ordinary human action. He has to persuade us that the actions and beliefs, of other people in earlier societies and different cultures, embody a claim to reason which we cannot avoid addressing because it arises in our every attempt at explanation and interpretation.

THE EVOLUTION OF SOCIETY AND CULTURE [2]

Habermas's theory of social evolution is, as we have seen, made explicit through his early reconstructions of historical materialism. It is spelled out more fully in his later work on communication. In order to preserve what is fundamental in the marxist legacy he must purge orthodox marxism of its prejudice that 'law, religion, and morality have no history' — because, as the orthodoxy would have it, they are merely secondary manifestations of economic modes of production. Habermas wants to press the opposite view that the 'normative structures' [3] of culture, morality, and collective identity do not simply follow economic or system imperatives and that *they evolve according to their own logic*. He will be happy to agree with his many marxist associates that the developmental dynamics of these normative structures remain tied to 'economically conditioned systems problems' [4] and that, in this respect 'culture remains a superstructural phenomenon' [5]. Nonetheless, as we shall see, his bold intention is to 'defend the thesis that the development of these normative structures is the pacemaker of social evolution [6].

Habermas wants to make us keenly aware of the arbitrary element in any kind of theory that does not take stock of its own implicit assumptions with respect to time, history and evolution. In a passage that announces the purpose of his studies of social evolution he reminds us that [7]:

Assumptions about the organizational principle of society and about learning capacities and ranges of possible structural variation cannot be clearly checked empirically before historical developments have put the critical survival limits to the test. Evolutionarily oriented analyses of the present are always handicapped because they cannot view their object retrospectively. For that reason, theories of this type, whether Marxist or non-Marxist are forced to monitor their assumptions — assumptions that already underlie the delimitation and description of the object — on an instructive theory of social development. Characterizations of society as industrial, post-industrial, technological, scientific, capitalist, late-capitalist, state-monopolistic, state-capitalist, totally administered, tertiary, modern, post-modern, and so on, stem from just as many developmental models connecting the contemporary formation of society with earlier ones. In this regard, historical materialism can take on the task of determining the organizational principle of contemporary society from the perspective of the origin of this social formation — for example, with statements about the systems problems in the face of which traditional societies failed and about the innovations with which modern bourgeois society met the evolutionary challenges.

We are presented with, roughly speaking, three separate phases in the evolution of society, the first of which begins in the 'primitive' or 'neolithic' social formation. In these societies the organizational principle is basically the kinship system, i.e. the organization of primary sex and age roles. In this stage, society is a total institution and 'family roles simultaneously secure both system and social integration ... (through) ... worldviews (*Weltanschauungen*) and norms that are scarcely differentiated from one another' [8]. This is the point at which the cultural break with nature is first manifest in the very beginnings of a process of rationalization that is thereafter, so to speak, committed to its own partially independent and logically reconstructible process of development. This process, conceived in an unmistakably Hegelian way [9], begins as the rather particularistic and incoherent '"magical-animistic" representations of a mythology ... that ... first made possible the construction of a complex of analogies in which all natural and social phenomena were interwoven and could be transformed into one another' [10]. However, within these societies authority and belief are still largely inseparable and the crises that threaten the survival of society come not from within but rather from external changes that overload their social/familial structures and undermine tribal identities.

There follows what I shall, for the sake of convenience, condense into a second stage that begins with the transition (somewhere between the eighth and fourth century BC) from archaic civilizations, such as ancient Egypt, to 'developed civilizations' such as ancient Greece, China, and Rome etc. In these still-traditional societies, the principle of organization changes to class domination and, as the production and distribution of social wealth shifts away 'from familial forms of organization to ownership of the means of production', so the kinship system surrenders the central functions of power and control to the State [11]. From this stage on, there is an actual or latent tension between the imperatives of system integratation and those of social integration, or more loosely speaking, between social structure and culture. As the 'system' (which here means 'society'; but we shall, for the moment, continue using the systems language to show why Habermas has borrowed it [12]) evolves and achieves a higher level of internal differentia-tion, it is better able to cope with its environment (nature and other societies). But this enhanced 'steering capacity' is won at the cost of emerging internal conflict. From here onwards social integration will depend substantially on the *cultural sphere* and the degree to which worldviews can effectively *legitimate and rationalize* social institutions at a level that is adequate to maintain compliance and social cohesion. This evolutionary step has involved a raising of the *level of justification* which Habermas understands as: the formal conditions of the acceptability of grounds or reasons, conditions that lend to legitimations their efficacy, their power to produce consensus and shape motives [13].

For example, in ancient Egypt the pharaohs were represented as the god Horus or as Osiris, the guarantor of external existence in all things; or in the case of Tutankamen, as the son of Amun, who is represented as the source of the young king's strength and external life. The point is that, in this early stage, mythical narration was sufficient to justify the power of rulers. But with the development of the early imperial civilizatons of the middle dynasties of China, and of Rome and Greece, etc., we see the emergence of greater internal complexity and social differentiation, a more elaborated structure of domination, and hence a greater need for *legitima-tions* that is now met, at a higher level of justification, with cosmologically gounded ethics and higher religions and philosophies that assume a more clearly rationalized character and that are communicated as *dogmatized knowledge*. We are still in the early phases of what Habermas, with Weber, describes as 'traditional' societies in which authority (*Herrschaft*) is, of course, legitimated through tradition: the difference now is that these traditions are *increasingly rationalized*, and this means internally organized around unifying principles and professionally taught by priests and teachers.

These higher levels of justification are generally necessary to support more structurally elaborated but still pre-modern and traditional societies which have another defining characteristic inasmuch as they are organized through a more or less clearly differentiated *state* apparatus. With respect to the development of the normative structures another important corollary is that action is coordinated through an increasingly rationalized system of law. A crucial change has occurred inasmuch as the law is no longer Caesar's will but a *rationalized body of principles* against which Caesar may be judged. Moreover, as Habermas insists, the law must always by its very nature embody validity claims that are inseparably tied to the worldviews (to 'collective representations' and to the 'conscience collective', if you will) that we find manifest in collective identity and in all other normative structures. Habermas insists that legitimacy cannot, as in the positivist theory of law, shrink to pure legality; the law can never become an arbitrary instrument for the legitimation of anything and everything because it has an internal connection to truth claims that are, however, 'counter-factually', *inherent in the culture*. Again we have a proliferation of terms that he uses somewhat interchangeably, but the essential point is, I hope, clear: domination is indissolubly linked to culture and to a process of cultural rationalization that follows its own developmental logic and is manifest in an evolution of normative structures that set limits to what can and cannot be legitimated and thus used to achieve social integration.

Within this second stage there will be a further development of societies that are alredy firmly based on deeply institutionalized power/class structures, organized through a developed State, and legitimated through normative structures and cultural forms that are articulated and transmitted in a more rationalized way. Yet the rationalization of culture is still locked within ontologically grounded representations of the world; locked, that is to say, within a metaphysic that ascribes ultimate reality to God, Being, or Nature, and thus strictly circumscribes the scope of rational action and individual autonomy. Although Habermas's periodization is rather vague, he explains that in modern times (roughly from the late Renaissance to the eighteenth century) the 'status of ... [these] ... ultimate grounds becomes problematic, Classical natural law was reconstructed; the new theories of natural law that legitimated the emerging modern state claimed to be valid independently of cosmologies, religions, or ontologies' [14]. This signals a decisive further shift in the level of justification inasmuch as now, at the threshold of this third stage that is our own modern period [15],

> the ultimate grounds can no longer be made plausible ... (and hence) ... *the formal conditions of justification themselves obtain legitimating force* ... the level of justification has become reflective. The procedures and pre-suppositions of justification are

themselves now the legitimating grounds on which the validity of legitimation is based. The idea of an agreement that comes to pass among all parties, as free and equal, determines the procedural type of legitimacy of modern times.

In this formulation we have a fleeting glimpse into the centre of his political sociology. Indeed we see that the whole theory is designed to secure a strict *distinction between the form and the contents of social action.* The distinction (and the anthropological history through which it has been justified) accepts the multiplicity and the endless competition among value orientations that is so characteristic of modern societies: yet with this distinction the relativity of value contents is accepted without compromising the *non*-arbitrary and *rational* claim that arises in the forms of agreement, argumentation, and assessment etc.

Is it too early to tell whether Habermas has succeeded in translating Hegel's idealist and dialectical philosophy of history into a developmental theory of social evolution that is serviceable for modern social anthropology. Clearly the whole theory hangs on the plausibility of extremely abstract concepts of 'organizational principle' and 'level of justification'. Since philosophical anthropology was one of the earliest influences in Habermas's own intellectual development [16] we should not be surprised that he enters anthropological problems from his own German perspective and with the ulterior purpose of grounding these concepts as supports for a broader critical social theory of modern late capitalist sociey. They are indeed extremely abstract concepts, but no more so than the basic principles that Lévi-Strauss has given to the structuralist and post-structuralist anthropology that Habermas now means to address as a full competitor. Nor should we be moved by the complaints of British and American ethnographers who, with reckless courage, still believe in the intelligence of their own attempts to record the behaviour of 'natives' in exotic environments [17]. There is certainly something compelling in Habermas's claim that more internally differentiated and complex societies have a greater capacity for dealing with both internal and external changes than do those in which the 'organizational principle' is still tied to a mechanical solidarity. One excellent study [18] suggests that villagers in at least one small semi-tribal society, the Zamora, on the fringes of the cash ecomomy of the Philippines, have a more adaptable mode of reasoning and are much more able to differentiate between individual and collective interests than Habermas's theory would seem to allow. Yet there are very few such studies and, as others have observed [19], much more careful empirical interpretation is needed before any assessment can be made.

In this thumbnail sketch we see how Habermas constructs a theory of social evolution that turns a dialectical philosophy of history into a developmental theory of social evolution that is amenable to empirical assessment and application. Similarly, we see how the stages in Marx's economic history (his historical materialism) are correlated with a map to the stage-by-stage expansion of collective knowledge that is, again, amenable to empirical assessment in the light of historical and anthropological evidence.

With breathtaking boldness Habermas has added a third dimension to this part of the theory. He as done this by incorporating another developmental 'logic', taken this time from the cognitive psychology of Piaget, from psychodynamic theories of ego-development, and from Kohlberg's psychological theory of moral development [20]. Although there is no space here for a discussion of the specific points of convergence between the different categories involved, the basic thrust of Habermas's initiative [21] is clearly evident in the broad lines of the diagram shown in Fig. 2 [22].

Erik Erikson, justly the best-known of the American neo-Freudian 'ego-psychologists', outlines a developmental theory of psychosocial development that proceeds, in eight stages, from early infancy to old age [23] — in each stage the further development of the individual depends on a successful resolution of the conflicts that arise between the polarities that define each stage (in Erikson's work the best known of these is the polarity in adolescence between 'identity' and 'identity confusion'). In a similar way Piaget's cognitive psychology [24] posits three stages of cognitive development from 'pre-operational' thought, through 'concrete operational thought', to 'formal (= abstract) operational thought'. More interesting still, from Habermas's point of view, are Kohlberg's six stages in the development of moral consciousness. The first begins with a 'punishment/ obedience orientation' and it is socially correlated with an 'idea of the good and just life', that is at this level crudely geared only to the maximization of pleasure through simple obedience, and dependent on the social sanction of punishment. The intervening four stages follow a development progess through four more stages of moral development from 'instrumental hedonism', to 'the good by orientation', the 'law and order orientation', and then to a 'social-contractual legalism'. Habermas's *tour de force* is to correlate each stage of this individual psychological development at its own level in the ladder with validity claims that are matched and assimilated with successively rising *levels of justification* in his theory of *social* evolution. A developmental sequence is, of course, a teleological progress that points along a trend line, beyond the concrete social actuality of the here and now, to a higher potential, in a next stage, in which Reason is socially anchored in binding principles and set in 'universalized need interpretations', in 'complete reciprocity', and in an idea of 'the good and just life'

	Role Competence			Stages of Moral Consciousness			
Age level	Level of communication	Reciprocity requirement	Stages of moral consciousness	Idea of the good life	Domain of validity	Philosophical reconstruction	Age level
I	Actions and consequences of action	Incomplete reciprocity	1	Maximization of pleasure avoidance of pain through obedience	Natural and social environment		IIa
	Generalized pleasure/pain	Complete reciprocity	2	Maximization of pleasure — avoidance of pain through exchange of equivalents		Naive hedonism	
II	Roles — Culturally interpreted needs		3	Concrete morality of primary groups	Group of primary reference persons		
	Systems of norms — (Concrete duties)	Incomplete reciprocity	4	Concrete morality of secondary groups	Members of the political community	Concrete thought in terms of a specific order	IIb
III	Principles — Universalized pleasure/pain (utility)		5	Civil liberties, public welfare	All legal associates	Rational natural law	III
	Universalized duties	Complete reciprocity	6	Moral freedom	All humans as private persons	Formalistic ethics	
	Universalized need interpretations		7	Moral and political freedom	All as members of a fictive world society	Universal ethics of speech	

Fig. 2

based on moral and political freedon. This potentially rational future is, of course, the non-arbitrary touchstone, or 'counter-factual' standard, which Habermas will use, as we shall see, in his political sociology and in his theory of language, for his assessment of the irrationality of our own times. In short he claims to have successfully defined 'the ethically optimal end-point of moral development' [25], and to have joined a developmental theory of society with a process of psychological development that is, again, amenable to empirical assessment. In principle, at least, it grounds psychological development in society where it properly belongs. It 'operationalizes' the progress of reason in the process of psychological maturation, and prospectively it even offers academic psychologists all the exquisite possibilities of measurement!

FROM TRADITIONAL SOCIETY TO MODERNITY: THE RECONSTRUCTION OF MAX WEBER'S THEORY OF RATIONALIZATION

Explanations of the process of modernization lie at the very heart of the discipline of sociology and at the heart of every major social theory. Tönnies explained this passage from traditional to modern society as a shift from '*Gemeinschaft*' to '*Gesellschaft*'. For Durkheim it is a change from 'mechanical' to 'organic' solidarity. In Marx it is explained as a change in the mode of production. Although Habermas's theory encompasses all of these perspectives his reconstruction of Max Weber's theory of rationalization is, as we have already suggested, certainly one of its most essential constituents.

Recent historical research has made us more aware of our tendency both to romanticize the so-called 'traditional' societies of the Middle Ages and to underestimate their variability. In some (e.g. the early Italian cities) 'the state' was much more developed than in others; and there is a comparable variability of family structures, of church and religion, and of forms of production and economic dependency. Yet these were 'traditional societies' in something like the Weberian sense and in varying measure normatively regulated by the traditional authority of the 'eternal yester-year' in which I obey my father as he obeyed his father before him, and so on, in a fairly unchanging past in which the historical memory of ancestors shades into a panoply of religious symbols. Of course traditional societies are much more complicatd than this and, as social historians and anthropologists insist, they are also more conflict-ridden, more disordered, and perhaps even more 'individualistic' and competitive than we may have supposed. However, once all the qualifications have been made and accepted we are still faced with the double challenge of understanding these societies *and* of reconstructing the intervening transformations and changes that have led to 'modernity' and to 'modern' and late capitalist societies.

Why can't the problem of social rationalization and modernization be addressed directly without another journey into the basement, this time to the foundations of Weber's work? Habermas's answer is that Weber's theory of rationalization has a significance for the understanding of modernity that is quite fundamental. We pursue the problem of modernization through Max Weber because his 'mistakes' embody our own intellectual and practical helplessness in the face of our own age. He forces us to face the possibility that our values, and our choices about the things we value, may have lost any kind of meaningful or coherent relation to the objective world in which we still have to stitch our lives together. And when we try to look for some kind of historical orientation to our situation, his problem, and our problem, is that we fall between two stools as we founder between contradictory understandings of our past and of our possible futures. On the one hand, we are quite sure that the passage from traditional societies to our own has been a deliverance from magic, from witchcraft and sorcery, and from holy terrors of the many kinds that produced the Inquisition, poor Galileo's unhappy end, and the witches of Salem. This progress, together with the development of science, learning, technology and art is a *rational progress*. Weber calls it the process of 'disenchantment' and with him we evaluate it *positively*. On the other hand, when we bring the lens of history closer to our own time we see things very differently indeed. Suddenly the progress of learning turns into a semi-autonomous growth of science and technology [26] that takes us over and leads, not to an expansion of possibilities, but through a course that Habermas reconstructs under the rubrics of 'rationalization as the loss of meaning' and 'rationalization as the loss of freedom' — in short, a course that leads straight to the 'Iron Cage' of late capitalism. In this contradiction, past and present grind together in our present without any padding and produce a crisis of self-understanding for both the individual and the society.

This is the problem. Habermas tries to reconcile the two processes, of disenchantment and of rationalization, into a single theory of modernization and modernity. To do the job properly there has to be a reconstruction of Weber that 'takes the theory apart and puts it back together again in a new form in order to attain more fully the aim it has set for itself' [27].

Weber's theory of rationalization — Phase one: 'Disenchantment' or 'positive rationalization'

Although these discussions are inherently difficult because they are so abstract, our task is made somewhat easier in this first section because

Habermas largely shares Weber's view with respect to the origins of modernity. Indeed the purpose of this part of the reconstruction is to highlight and then to carry forward what Weber saw as a largely positive early development of 'occidental rationalization'. We are dealing here with an historical process that dates roughly from the European High Middle Ages to the eighteenth century. During this period there is a progressive institutionalization of higher levels of rationality. In terms of our discussion in the preceding section, there is a change in 'the organizational principle' of society and a corresponding release and realizaton of 'expanded possibilities of learning' and development. This progress is achieved through three interlocking developments, namely (a) the emergence of what Weber called the 'Protestant Ethic', (b) the differentiation among others of the spheres of science, religion and art, and (c) emergence of post-conventional modern law. I shall discuss each of these in turn.

(1)   *The Protestant Ethic*
Weber's sociology of religion is certainly the best developed, and perhaps even the most important part, of his unfinished work. Had he lived only a little longer we would not now mistakenly read *Economy and Society* as his definitive work. Instead, as Habermas with Tenbruck [28] and others insists, we would have seen that Weber means to explain the rationalization process principally as an outgrowth of a unique and particular religious orientation to the world of Luther and Calvin, and of ascetic protestantism in general. All the other world religions and especially those of China and of India tended to reinforce, and even to sanctify, traditional action, behaviour and custom [29]. By contrast the unique feature of ascetic protestantism is that it breaks the constraints of tradition and *transforms ordinary worldly action and behaviour*. It does so most especially in the crucially important area of economic and entrepreneurial activity. Habermas uses this marvellous paragraph from Weber to point to the inner logic of this religiously inspired transformation [30]:

> Only the vocational ethic of ascetic Protestantism produced a principled, systematic and unbroken unity of an inner-worldly vocational ethic with the assurance of religious salvation .... This inner-worldly asceticism has a number of characteristics and consequences not found in any other religion. It demanded of the believer not celibacy, as in the case of the monk, but the elimination of all erotic pleasure or desire; not poverty, but the elimination of all idle enjoyment of unearned wealth and income, and the avoidance of all feudalistic, life-loving ostentation of wealth; not

the ascetic death-in-life of the cloister, but an *alert, rationally controlled conduct of life* and the avoidance of all surrender to the beauty of the world, to art, or to one's own moods and emotions. The clear and uniform goal of this asceticism was *the disciplining and methodological organization of conduct*. Its typical representative was the 'man of vocation' [Berufsmensch]; and its specific result was the *rational, functional organization of social relations*.

Habermas pays scant attention to the potentially fatal challenges of marxists and empiricist historians who argue predictably, but with some force, that both he and Weber read the problem upside-down and that the Protestant Ethic was caused more by changes in the material conditions of economy and production rather than the other way about [31]. Habermas will insist that religious *culture* or, in Weber's language, 'ideal interests' rather than 'material interests', are, in this context, the principal engine of social, structural, and economic transformation. From out of this initially purely religious culture comes an all-important catalyst for this process of occidental rationalization; namely, 'the methodical conduct of life'.

The 'methodical conduct of life' is so important because, as we shall see, it embodies the highest form of rationality, namely 'practical rationality'. This is the highest form — and it is only the *form* and not the content that matters — because it joins and reconciles ends/means or 'purposive rationality (*Zweckrationalität*) with value-rationality (*Wertrationalität*) into a single life-form with universal significance.

In this way, as we shall see later, the 'methodical conduct of life' and Weber's very undeveloped idea of practical rationality point, in Habermas's reconstructions, to our contemporary situation with at least some outlines for a response to the problems of our modernity. For Weber, of course, the reconciliation of subjective experience with the objective world was a solitary personal struggle with fate. Although Habermas will recast the problem into the fully dialogical and social terms of his theory of 'communicative rationality' the importance of these Weberian constituents must not be underestimated.

(2) *The differentiation of cultural spheres of value and action*

As the process of 'disenchantment' proceeds from the high Middle Ages onwards, we know that the old religious or 'magical–animistic' representations of the world gradually break up — that is what 'disenchantment' means — and their spellbinding power is lost. Out of this comes what Weber calls a differentiation of cultural orders and spheres of value. The basic point is really quite simple. As these pre-modern traditional societies of Europe grow larger and more complex there is an increasing 'specialization' and differentiation of those spheres of activity that Weber idenfities as political activity, art, religion, intellectual development, economic activity and even the pursuit of erotic pleasure. Weber emphasizes that in the course of this differentiation each of these spheres becomes 'autonomous' [32] and this simply means that, gradually, each sphere is regulated by axioms and norms that are increasingly incommensurate with those of the others.

There is no clear symmetry in Weber's work between the cultural and institutional facets of this process of differentiation. He wants to deal in one way with a cultural proliferation of different and competing worldviews (*Weltanschauungen*) and in a different way with the differentiation of institutions (religious, economic and political etc.) and of the normative structures that crystallize around them. As is usual with these reconstructions, Habermas takes what he deems most essential and then walks away from the rest. In this case, with a boldness that seems almost to embarrass him [33], he comes up with the reconstructed argument that the religious tradition gives rise, at the threshold of modernity, to a differentiation between *three basic orientations to the world* — and again, in these categories, we recognize the recurring and fundamental threefold scheme of Habermas's work.

In the *first* place, Habermas argues, the methodical pursuit of purposes leads, as the magic is cast off, to an ever clearer and more disciplined development and application of 'instrumental', 'ends/means' or 'rational–purposive' action (these are all different English translations for the German '*zweckrational*'). This leads, of course, to the development of science and technology in semi-autonomous universities and academies.

Secondly, we see a similar development of ethics and morality. Again, as the magic and the traditional shroudings are thrown off, so ethics are increasingly rationalized. Formal principles and norms take the place of the cruder traditional moral prescriptions, proscriptions, and sanctions of the the tribe, the clan, and the religious community. Moreover the principles now have to be applied *universalistically*, to each strictly according to the rule and without fear or favour.

Third, as every visitor to an art gallery cannot fail to notice, late Renaiassance art — and music and literature as well — breaks free of the exclusively religious traditions of the Middle Ages. In this aesthetic expressive domain there is a parallel differentiation from religion and science. The aesthetic sphere achieves a certain institutionalized autonomy as art works are bought and sold in the market and as its methods are formalized and taught in 'schools' according to principles. Accordingly it too moves into a course of progressive *rationalization*.

(3) Law and justice

Habermas's complaint is that Weber's sociology of religion does not fit with his sociology of law. His reconstructions are designed to show, with the help of Schluchter [34] and of other Germans, that the rationalization of law is not driven by the functional requirements of the state but rather that it is propelled by the inner logic of the rationalization of culture and of ethics. It is clear that from the Middle Ages onwards the law achieves a certain autonomy from the church and from the political will of kings, princes, clerics, and potentiates. It is increasingly controlled, taught, and professionalized by specialist jurists. With the development of jurisprudence, the teaching and application of the law becomes ever more reflective. As the inner logic unfolds, tradition, custom, and religious dogma are progressively eliminated in favour of formal principles that are applied with a broadening internal consistency. In short, the law is rationalized according to the same *increasingly universalistic principles* that guide the historical development of culture and of ethics. Habermas insists that it must have been at least as important as the Protestant Ethic in calling in the development of the modern world [35].

Weber's theory of rationalization — Phase two: The 'Iron Cage'

Mommsen certainly chose an apt phrase when he described Weber as 'a despairing liberal'. Weber despairs because the process of rationalization, 'at the other end' of the Protestant Ethic, leads only to the 'Iron Cage' of late capitalism that he describes with the following well-known words [36]:

> The Puritan wanted to work in a calling; we are forced to do so. For when asceticism was carried out of monastic cells into everyday life, and began to dominate worldly morality, it did its part in building the tremendous cosmos of the modern economic order. This order is *now bound to the technical and economic conditions of machine production which to-day determine the lives of all the individuals who are born into this mechanism*, not only those directly concerned with economic acquisition, *with irresistible force.* Perhaps it will so determine them until the last ton of fossilized coal is burnt. In Baxter's view the care for external goods should only lie on the shoulders of the 'saint like a light cloak, which can be thrown aside at any moment'. But fate decreed that the cloak should become an iron cage.

The 'Iron Cage' becomes the symbol of modernity, of late capitalism, and of a rationalization that Weber now conceives *in a completely negative way*. Habermas wants us to take a second look at this scenario: he wants to show us that, in contrast with Weber's analysis of this first phase of the rationalization process, there has been a *shift and a narrowing* in Weber's perspective.

The shift of perspective is clearer still in this typical passage in which Weber pinpoints the situation of workers in the new order of late-capitalism. According to Weber we discover in the case of workers in every field [37]:

> This all-important economic foundation: *the 'separation' of the worker from the material means of operation* — from the means of production in the economy, from the means of war in the military, from the means of administration in public administration, from the means of research in universities and laboratories, and from financial means in all these cases — *is the common and decisive basis of the modern state* in its political, cultural and military operations *and of the private capitalist economy*.

To make the thrust still clearer Habermas follows with another extract from Weber [38].

> In a historical perspective too, the 'progress' towards the bureaucratic state, adjudication and administering according to rationally established laws and regulations, is very closely related to modern capitalist development. The modern capitalist enterprise rests (internally) primarily on calculation. It requires for its existence a legal and administrative system whose functioning *can be rationally calculated, at least in principle, on the basis of fixed general norms, just like the expected performance of a machine*.

Now the shift in Weber's perspective is clear. The rationalization process is no longer primarily a cultural and 'psychological' process: we are no longer tracing a process that unfolds, as it did before, in the dimensions of *culture* and *personality*. The perspective has changed, and it is now the functional imperatives of the state and the economy that together drive the rationalization process in a gloomy path that leads ultimately to spiritual, intellectual, and moral extinction. In Weber's view it is a process in which the original ethical and religious–cultural motivations are dissolved into a 'pure utilitarianism' [39]. It is this entirely negative course of development that fuses with the neo-marxist diagnosis of late capitalism as the 'commodification of everything'. As we have seen, it establishes the perspective for most of the critical theorists of the Frankfurt School and is summed up in the two theses of 'rationalization as the loss of meaning' and 'rationalization as the loss of freedom'.

Habermas wants to stress that the changed perspective is also a *narrowed* perspective because Weber is now looking at the rationalized process *only* in terms of the 'one-sided' institutionalization of rational–purposive (*zweckrational*) action: one-sided because it is assumed that value-rational (*wertrational*) action just fades away into extinction. In short, as Habermas puts it, the reference point from which Weber investigates societal rationalization is, therefore, the purposive rationality of entrepreneurial activity [40].

The rationalization process 'reconstructed'
With the key to a room with one of the very best views we re-emerge from the basement. For the sake of convenience the two phases of the passage from traditional (European) societies to the modern late capitalist societies may be diagrammatically represented as in Fig. 3.

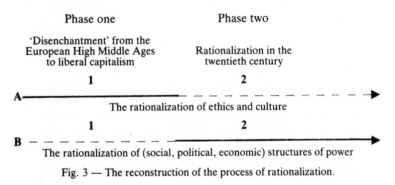

Fig. 3 — The reconstruction of the process of rationalization.

We can now better understand Weber's mighty contribution, his 'mistakes', and the thrust of Habermas's reconstruction. The problem is that Weber's account of the rationalization process is incomplete, discontinuous, and inconsistent. As we have seen, Weber's focus moves along the two (solid) lines A1 and B2. Weber's analysis of the first (phase one) of the rationalization process is cast in terms of an unfolding logic of development in the realm of culture and ethics (along line A1). The mistake and the inconsistency arise in the discontinuity of the explanatory framework as Weber 'switches tracks' in the shift from the first to a second phase that he thereafter 'one-sidedly' explains in terms of the social and structural institutionalization of power in the economy and the state (line B2).

Against this background we see more clearly the thrust and the purpose of Habermas's reconstruction. In order to resolve Weber's outlines into a fully-fledged theory of rationalization, constructed as a world-historical process with a truly universal significance, Habermas must take apart the unfinished work and then fill in and expand the two incomplete or misconstrued aspects of the larger project, namely A2 and B1.

A few comments must suffice to explain what Habermas does to fill in the part of the theory represented in the figure as B1. It is important to stress Habermas's view that Marx and Weber are essentially complementary to each other. With this conviction Habermas argues that interests and ideas are of *equal* importance in shaping the course of history and rationalization [41]. Although he certainly wants to take sides against the positivist reading of Weber and to stress, here as elsewhere, that culture and ethics are 'the pacemakers' of social evolution he will go only part of the way with what he calls 'culturalist' (a euphemism for 'idealist') explanations that would, certainly for example in Tenbruck's extremely Hegelian reading, reduce every development in the social structural 'base' (line B) to a purely cultural dynamic (in line A). Habermas offers little more than a few fairly perfunctory acknowledgements that Weber's explanations of this first phase are developed 'from above' and therefore lack the complementary *causal* explanations that must come from the dimension below. The marxist dimension is missing at least in part because it is taken for granted and pursued in other texts [42].

Perhaps the main thrust in this otherwise rather thin part of the reconstruction is Habermas's insistence that the neglected and important development in this path (B1) is *the development of the law*. There is a continuity along this (B1: B2) inasmuch as the nucleus of the modern state and economy develop early in the structures of civil law and public justice. The blade of Habermas's argument is aimed at positivist and functionalist interpretations that try always to depict the law merely as a completely malleable instrument of power and interest. It does, of course, serve power interests and it is indeed used as a cruel instrument of repression, but Habermas's point is that the *form* of 'post-traditional' law, from about the sixteenth century, embodies a logic of cultural and ethical development that *sets ever more coherent limits to what it can and cannot legitimate.* Through the law, power is therefore constrained by cultural and ethical 'principles' that lie beyond its reach and, for an understanding of *society,* this is of equal importance to other faces of the law as a medium through which culture and ethics are neutralized and appropriated in the service of power [43]. In the course of history, as now, legal structures mediate between ideas and interests in *both* directions.

The centrepiece and the *raison d'être* of the whole reconstruction is, clearly, the explanation of the neglected course that continues in A2, and equally, of the 'dialectic' in modernity (between A and B) of culture, ideas and ethics on the one hand, with structures of power and interest on the other. Here Habermas has established, this time through his reconstruction of Weber, that the evolution of society proceeds along *two paths* (A and B) and through the '*dialectic*' *between culture and structure*, or, in Weber's language, between 'ideal' and 'material' interests. With respect to our own era the thrust of the argument is, of course, that the rationalization process continues along a course anchored in the past and projected through our own time into a future that is therefore *potentially* more rational, and, further, that culture and ethics continue at least potentially and, so to speak 'in the abstract', along the line (A2). This means that the on-going dialectic of culture and ethics with the structures of power (in B2) *continues*, if only potentially, and again, 'in the abstract'. Weber's mistake was to see the relation between these two courses *not* as a dialectical progress but rather as the one-sided assimilation and institutionalization, into the structures of the economy and the state, *only* of the 'purposive–rational' (*zweckrational*) reason of science and technology. If we mistakenly accept this one-sided institutionalization we then wrongly assume with Weber that the ethical and cultural springs of action just rot away and can no longer have any 'rationally motivating force' or any further 'structure-forming effects'. The future, and with it autonomy, will and consciousness, all disappear into the Iron Cage and the blind career of the 'machine'.

In case we ever doubted it we can again see why Habermas is so difficult. His reconstruction of Weber, and with it his whole work, ask us to look into our own post-modern future through a dialectic, and along a trendline between two paths (A and B) of which one, the structures of power and economy, press in upon our lives with an overwhelming immediacy, whereas the other (line A) is, in opposite measure, dimly visible, heavily repressed, elusive and manifest for the most part only 'in the abstract' and as a beckoning potentiality of open possibilities. In effect, he seems to be asking us to take up a viewpoint in between two fields of grossly disproportionate strength and immediacy.

The inner logic of culture, ethics (A2) and worldviews in which they are manifest, is carried forwards in at least two respects that deserve some concluding comment. In the first place the disenchantment and rationalization of tradition moves forward (into A2) in two ways, not one. The advance of those 'cognitive' or 'rational–purposive' structures of consciousness with such conspicuously visible 'structure-forming effects' (in such areas as science and technology, entrepreneurial activity, bureaucracy etc.) is, according to Habermas, *necessarily linked* in our structures of consciousness, to a similar progress in the 'inner logic' of ethics and morality. Here I think the aim of Habermas's reconstruction is to chart, as follows, a course that begins first with the advance of the Protestant Ethic beyond tradition-bound ethics and then secondly (along line A2) beyond a 'legalistic ethic' to, thirdly, an 'ethics of conviction' that leads then to 'an ethics of responsibility'. In other writings Habermas will trace the development differently. But here, and with respect specifically to Weber, Habermas argues that the Protestant Ethic starts off a development that leads logically, in its form and structure, to a 'universalistic ethics of brotherhood' [44].

He wants to argue that these very abstract formal developments in the sphere of ethics and ideas contain, stored up in their inner logic, practical consequences that are directly analogous to, and just as significant as, those that are stored up in scientific theories. Just as extremely abstract advances in theoretical science, such as, for example, the paradigm shift to relativity theory in physics, open possibilities and have direct consequences in the concrete achievements of science and technology, so also do these equally abstract developments in worldviews ethics and culture contain, in the same way, a store of practical consequences with potentially 'structure-forming effects' for the institutionalization of an increasing measure of justice, truth and freedon. Their 'inner logic' selectively favours the legitimation of social and political structures with a *universalist promise*. And there we have a glimpse of the political sociology that will follow in Chapter 4.

METHOD AND MEANING

As we have seen, in Habermas's own German language and tradition the very notion of natural science (*Naturwissenschaft*) calls up a matching term — *Geisteswissenschaften* — for which we have absolutely no English equivalent. 'Human sciences'?, 'Sciences of consciousness'?, 'Science of the Spirit'?, 'Science of the Idea'?, 'Human and cultural sciences of the Mind'? Every attempt at an English translation produces an ugly contrivance that makes one wince, and this bears testimony to the iron grip (the clumsy pun must be forgiven) of traditional empiricism upon our conceptual vocabulary. These remarks serve only to remind us again that in the English-speaking world we are used to looking at the social sciences against the background of the natural sciences and that our analytic philosophers (the sanitary inspectors of traditional empiricism) have almost succeeded in banishing larger notions of cultrue and meaning to the Continent. But of course this will not do: apart from anything else it is bad science.

Our problem is, of course, that a philosophically informed and methodologically self-conscious social science must give up the illusion that we can enjoy some vantage point that is somehow outside society, history, culture and the individual. There is no external reference point which guarantees objectivity or provides a basis for 'presuppositionless description'. Nor is there any ready methodologically guaranteed line between observer and observed, author and text, knowledge and interpretation, fact and value, or between explanation and understanding. Yet this problem does not entitle us to sink into a relativism that merely dissolves social reality into the opinions of its participants. We must instead face a fundamental ambiguity of the human condition in which there is, like it or not, an interpenetration of subject and object and a situation in which, 'the other is there both as an object for me and as another subject with me' [5]. It is on this ground that Habermas takes up the challenge of rebuilding a methdology that can join internal and external validity and there establish surer methodological foundations.

With these problems in mind we are faced with the question, What are these worldviews and traditions that we see evolving in history and what is our relation to them? To maintain a broadly sociological focus I shall avoid the large philosophical questions and offer some brief comments on two topics that go to the heart of Habermas's methodological discussions.

Lifeworld (*Lebenswelt*) and worldview

'Lifeworld' (*Lebenswelt*) is the key methodological term in Habermas's later work. It is in the lifeworld that social and economic structures interpenetrate with action and consciousness. The lifeworld is the substratum of our conscious worldviews (*Weltanschauungen*) and of all social action. Roughly speaking, worldviews share the same relation to the lifeworld for Habermas as the Conscious does to the Unconscious for Freud. Just as Freud saw the conscious life of the ego as a fragmentary and partial expression of a great storehouse of forgotten but ever-active experience in the Unconscious, so also Habermas, in a similar way, argues that the lifeworld 'stands behind the back of each participant in communication'. In phenomenological terms the lifeworld comprises that vast stock of taken-for-granted definitions and understandings of the world that give coherence and direction to our everyday actions and interactions. It is, as Habermas reminds us, 'so unproblematic that we are simply incapable of making ourselves conscious of this or that part of it at will' [46]. He sometimes refers to the lifeworld as the 'background consensus of everyday life' and often as the 'storehouse of knowledge' that is passed from one generation to the next. There is no vantage point of observation that is outside the lifeworld: we cannot step out of our lifeworld. With the help of this concept Habermas is able on the one hand to distance himself from functionalist notions of socialization that are usually articulated in terms of roles, rewards and sanctions, and on the other, to rework the very idea of socialization in terms of *mutual learning*, gradually achieved within the expanding horizons of a lifeworld.

With argument and reflection we can relate to our lifeworld in a more ordered and rational way — that is partly what rationalization will mean. Yet the sheer difficulty of laying hold of this or that aspect of our lifeworld reminds us again and again of its primacy. The lifeworld sets the 'context-forming horizon' of social action and consciousness. To say therefore that this or that social structure is 'institutionalized' is just another way of saying that it structures there our conscious actions and worldviews (*Weltanschauungen*). As we grub our way down through the conscious layers of the lifeworld our every effort at self-understanding sooner or later comes up against its unyielding structural constraints; constraints that coordinate many of our social actions without our knowledge and 'behind our backs' from within those reaches of the lifeworld that lie beyond the threshold of consciousness.

The *Lebenswelt* concept adds a methodological dimension to the discussion, in the preceding section, of Habermas and Weber. Firstly, it helps clarify the reconstruction of Weber's process of rationalization. Our overly formal image of a rationalization process projected into infinity along two rails is made good with these methodological concepts of lifeworld and worldview. We see now that the interaction between culture, ethics and consciousness (line A in Fig. 3), on the one hand, and social structures (line B), on the other, is manifest in the lifeworld. That is also where we find the 'seam' between social action and social structure. These processes have an empirical locus and so Habermas escapes the stereotypical criticism that he is merely another idealist who conjures up the social world in a metaphysic or a cosmology that he has plucked out of the ether.

Similarly, we can now see more clearly what Habermas means when he says that the reconstruction must, with Weber's words, simultaneously support explanations both 'from above' and 'from below'. All significant social events and processes are directly or indirectly reflected in the lifeworld and have to be assessed and understood there from two perspectives. In the first place, we must enter social reality 'from above' through interpretations of the '*Weltanschauungen*' of those people whose lives we seek to understand. These interpretations of worldviews succeed when they are, again in Weber's words, 'adequate at the level of meaning'. But Habermas is not an idealist because he insists that every explanation from above must be supplemented with an explanation 'from below' and so in terms of the structural context of the lifeworld — to which marxists refer as the 'base', in contradistinction to 'superstructure'. From this perspective the social scientist must step beyond interpretation and *explain* how the objective and material environment — social, economic and physical — produces this or that change or disturbance in the lifeworld. And so from this perspective our explanations of social actions and world views also achieve, in Weber's other term, an 'adequacy at the level of cause'.

Similarly, we see that the lifeworld and worldview concepts open the way to some further clarification of the rationalization process. In a nutshell: Habermas wants us to *study the evolution of society as the rationalization of the lifeworld.*

In traditional societies, worldviews (and contexts of action and interpretation) are more or less completely fixed in the spell of religious cosmologies and, at the same time, the stuctural correlates of the lifeworld are fixed in traditional kinship structures and in the economic structures of subsistence agricultural production. Under these circumstances the background convictions that guide interaction and communication come into play in a highly reified and 'nature-like' way. Of course, all sorts of ambiguities and negotiations can and do go on within the norms and cultrual structures that arise in this type of lifeworld: the point is that, at the lowest level of rationalization, the lifeworld charges social norms and cultural structures with a spellbinding force that blocks off further learning and change. 'To the degree that the lifeworld of a social group is interpreted through a mythical worldview, the burden of interpretation is removed from the individual member' [47]. Everything is understood holistically and agreements and understandings are ascribed rather than achieved.

By contrast, in our own more modern developed societies the rationalization of the 'base' (economy and state etc.) has allowed a greater rationalization of the lifeworld that is manifest in several different ways. Clearly the cultural tradition now contains formal concepts that allow fairly stable differentiations between the objective, social and subjective dimensions of our world. Similarly we find specialized languages that first allow and then 'deepen' evaluative criticism in all three cognitive, moral, and aesthetic dimensions of the cultural tradition [48]. Most importantly we find that, as this rationalization of the lifeworld proceeds, increasingly *reflective* and *critical* processes of evaluation gradually dissolve those elements of the cultural tradition that were once dogmatically ascribed. It is in this way, according to Habermas, that 'expanded possibilities for learning' are 'released'. The point that must not be missed is that rationalization is a function *not* of the *contents* of the cultural tradition but rather of the new possibilities of criticizing them that are now 'institutionalized' in a progressively more *rationalized* lifeworld.

Habermas and hermeneutics

It is against the background of the German humanities tradition (the *Geisteswissenschaften*) that Weber and then Habermas, among others, address the problem of how it is that we come to *understand* (*verstehen*) those webs of meaning that we call traditions. As we know, Weber and those who have followed him insist that meanings and traditions are understood with means that are categorically different from the methods that we use to explain events in the physical world. But how do we grasp and justify the *methods* for the interpretation of meanings? Although these questions are taken up in the new context of Habermas's developed theory of language, many of his most basic methodological standpoints were first formed in his dialogue with Hans Georg Gadamer and with philosophical hermeneutics. Gadamer was a student of Heidegger and is to the present day the most important voice in German hermeneutics, a branch of scholarship that concerns itself exclusively with the interpretation of texts and cultural artefacts. This otherwise obscure branch of scholarship therefore becomes important because, among other reasons, it provides Habermas with a key for the understanding of meanings and traditions: it offers the best route into the problems we face in framing, with Weber and Habermas, explanations of cultural phenomena — explanations that are 'adequate at the level of meaning'. I shall try to summarize in five points what Habermas takes from hermeneutics.

(1) Hermeneutics teaches us that meanings as such can only be understood 'from the inside out' and that 'the interpreter can elucidate this meaning or symbolic expression only as a virtual participant in the process of reaching understanding among those immediately involved' [49]. Both Gadamer and Habermas agree that the process of under-standing — of a tradition, a culture, or a text — requires a special kind of dialogical engagement with the mental world of the other person, the other culture, or the other tradition. Both stress that this is an *inter-subjective* process. I project my 'pre-understanding' — my prejudices, and my taken-for-granted assumptions — into the lifeworld of these villagers, in this or that early Renaissance society, in order to make sense of what the stonemasons were building in the village square or of what the funeral ceremony means for the participants — without my own 'pre-understanding' their social actions would be nothing more than completely incomprehensile physical movements. In explaining what happens in this process of interpretation Habermas is happy to borrow Gadamer's metaphor of a 'fusion of horizons'. Every situation involves a 'horizon' — my horizon is the encircling limit of my understanding. Just as I have my own horizon so also does a community a culture, and a tradition [50] have its own encircling horizon of meanings. The methodologically important point is that I understand the community, culture or tradition only in the 'moment' of doubt, dialogue, and question, that arises as my horizon meets the horizon that encircles the object of interpretation, be it a person, a culture, a text.

or, to take the paradigm case, a tradition. In the *fusion of the two horizons* translation is possible and a continuity of meaning and a common bond is established between the tradition and the interpreter. In that moment the tradition claims the interpreter who also, in some measure, makes the tradition his or her own — 'the interpreter is of the same fabric of tradition as his object' [51]. It is in this way that traditions evolve and pass from one generation to the next. The interpretation of tradition therefore *points beyond purely methodological considerations and illuminates the process of social and cultural reproduction.* At the same time as it defies empiricist explanations of society, culture, and personality it shows again that such human artefacts as traditions have to be understood 'from the inside out', from the point of view of a participant, and in Weber's terms, as 'meaningful social *action*'.

(2) In the 'fusion of horizons' there is a methodological and epistemological lesson that we would miss entirely if we misunderstood the process of interpretation as some kind of gratuitous or 'private' mental event. On the contrary, as Gadamer insists [52]:

> Such self-transposition is neither the empathetic projection of one individuality into another nor the subjection of the other to one's own standards; it means, rather, rising to a higher level of generality on which not only one's own particularity but that of the other is overcome. The concept of horizon presents itself here because it expresses the superior farsightedness that the one who is understanding must possess. To acquire a horizon means that one learns to see beyond the near and the all-too-near not in order to overlook it but in order better to see it in a larger whole and with a more accurate sense of its proportions.

There are at least three points that Habermas will seize from this and similar arguments. The first is that the 'fusion of horizons' and indeed the process of interpretation itself leads, at least methodologically, to an interpretation that is more inclusive, more comprehensive, 'deeper', and, in short, potentially *more rational* than whatever was possible before. Within the method there is a rational progress that points towards Reason (of course Hegel is smiling in the wings!). The second point is that the process of hermeneutic understanding leads the interpreter beyond his or her idiosyncratic 'private' understanding into a more *consensual* world of meaning that is ever *more public* and, in short, more readily communicable among an *ever-widening circle of interpreters*. The third point is that inasmuch as the fusion of horizons establishes a continuity of experience it also *orients the actions of the interpreter* and preserves the continuity of 'action-orienting under-standing' from one generation to the next and from one culture to the next.

(3) From the methodology that we use in the interpretation of texts and traditions, we learn something else that is of universal significance for all social scientific enquiry, namely that meaning and validity *are internally connected and arise together in the process of interpretation.* Here again Habermas uses hermeneutic interpretation as a favoured weapon against the empiricist assumption that we can read and eva-luate meaning and tradition against independent, 'presuppositionless', criteria of validation, for example, criteria taken from independent formal scientific methodological rules, from techniques of measure-ment, and from rules of ethnographic description etc. Habermas insists that 'only to the extent that the interpreter grasps the *reasons* that allow the author's utterance to appear as rational does he understand what the author could have *meant*' [53]. Successful interpretation is not won through some condescending attitude of 'open-mindedness' or of 'hermeneutic charity'. The point is that unless you, the would-be interpreter, take up *their* reasons 'virtually in the attitude of a partici-pant' you don't understand a damn thing! Yet, of course, this does not mean that the interpreter must accept the reasons of the sorcerer or the shaman. On the contrary, 'The interpreter absolutely cannot present reasons to himself without judging them, without taking a positive or negative position on them' [54].

Again the point is that the moment of successful interpretation is not just a warming aesthetic experience; it is also, of necessity, that moment where my reasons engage with their reasons. The continuity of experience that is established with every successful act of interpretation is always, tacitly if not explicitly, a stream of agreements and disagree-ments that appeal to *reasons*.

(4) Habermas's debate with Gadamer is exemplary because 'it offers privileged access to the unresolved problem of the origins of values' [55]. Once again, hermeneutics seems to provide sure arguments against another empiricist prejudice that values are more or less arbitrarily chosen, or that they are merely passions or habits. In Habermas's view, the methodology of hermeneutics has a universal importance inasmuch as it illuminates how norms pass historically from one generation to the next (and contemporaneously from one culture or social group to another). It shows how the process of interpreting and understanding a tradition involves an internalization of the value configurations that are part and parcel of its meaning. As a continuity of experience with the past is established in the moment of understand-

ing, traditions endow values with *authority*. This, in a nutshell, is how norms become effective in orienting social action with obligatory force. But, as we shall see, this does not justify Gadamer's view that traditions, once understood, have an indissoluble authority. For the moment it is enough to see that from the methodology of hermeneutics we can begin to penetrate what is otherwise the terrible dilemma that Ricoeur skillfully recalls as follows: 'If values are not our work but precede us, why do they not suppress our freedom? And if they are our work, why are they not arbitrary choices?' [56].

(5) The important influence of hermeneutics in Habermas's work is nowhere more visible than in the 'linguistic turn' of his later work. Habermas agrees with Gadamer that 'language is not only an object in our hands, it is the reservoir of tradition and the medium in and through which we exist' [57]. It is largely true that 'reality happens in language'. Socialization and cultural reproduction goes on through the medium of language. Ego-identity is formed and reciprocally stabilized in linguistic interaction.Social action is typically accomplished and coordinated through ordinary speech — we could go on. It is for these reasons that Habermas has taken on the colossal task of transposing his sociology and social theory into the paradigm of linguistic communication.

Habermas's affinity with philosophical hermeneutics is overshadowed by a fundamental objection that has been very eloquently articulated in the debate with Gadamer. Habermas agrees that it makes good sense to conceive of language as a kind of 'meta-institution on which all social institutions are dependent; for social action is constituted only in ordinary communication' [58]. Yet hermeneutics does not go far enough: it is insufficiently objective. By entering social reality only through the mutuality of understanding 'hermeneutics comes up against the walls of tradition from the inside as it were' [59]. The problem is that language is also a medium of power and oppression; language has an *ideological dimension*. As we see only too clearly in even casual observations of family relations and political culture, the most sincere efforts at understanding often serve only to tighten the grip of ideologically laden ascriptions of roles and responsibilities. Power relations institutionalized in language come upon us, as we shall see in the next chapter, as a 'systematically distorted' communication. A critical theory of society must therefore also provide objective explanations of social reality that come so to speak, 'from the outside in'. Again the problem with hermeneutics is that it affirms the 'rights' of tradition at the expense of reflection, at the expense of a potentially emancipatory reflection that proves itself [60], in being able to reject the claims of tradition .... Reflection dissolves substantiality because it not only confirms, but also breaks up, dogmatic forces. Authority and knowledge do not converge .... The right of reflection demands that the hermeneutic approach restrict itself. It calls for a reference system that goes beyond the framework of tradition as such: only then can tradition also be criticised'.

These considerations remind us of the preceding discussions. The limits of hermeneutics are those same limits beyond which 'culturalist' interpretation must give way to explanations that come 'from below', and take account of social structures that shape the lifeworld 'from the outside in' and which do not yield to hermeneutic understanding. Only a critical social theory can get at these deeper structres of power.

NOTES

[1] Jürgen Habermas, 'A Philosophico-Political Profile', *New Left Review,* **151**, 1985, pp. 75–105, see p. 101.

[2] Much of this section is based on a chapter of mine 'Habermas: Reason and the Evolution of Culture' that is to be published shortly by Allen & Unwin in a book edited by Diane Austin under the title *Creating Culture.*

[3] This is a generic term that Habermas sometimes uses interchangeably with 'collective identity', 'moral representations', 'the background consensus of everyday life', worldviews (*Weltanschauungen*), and 'lifeworld' (*Lebenswelt*). It is roughly equivalent in many usages with Durkheim's 'collective representations'.

[4] *Communication and the Evolution of Society* (hereafter CES), Chs 3 and 4.

[5] CES, p. 98.

[6] CES, p. 120.

[7] CES, pp. 126–127.

[8] *Legitimation Crisis,* trans. and introd. by T. McCarthy, Beacon Press, Boston, 1975; Heinemann, London, 1976, p. 18. (Hereafter LC.)

[9] In the dialectical progress of the Absolute Idea in Hegel's philosophy of religion through six progressively more rationally self-conscious stages from primitive religion, in which there is no differentiation between consciousness and Nature, to the final stage where religion is transcended by philosophy in which Reason is perfectly actualized, see Hegel's *Encyclopedia.*

[10] CES, p. 104.

[11] LC, p. 19.

[12] Many of these arguments are, as we shall see in the next chapter, taken from Niklas Luhmann who argues, in a very functionalist way, that internal differentiation is the surest path for the evolution of social systems and that it enhances the capacity for survival and effective control over the external environment, because it allows for 'the containment of disturbances in one "sub-system" and so prevents them from spreading like fire in a box of matches from one to all the others'. See Niklas Luhmann, *The Differentiation of Society*, Columbia University Press, New York, 1982, esp. Ch. 10.

[13] CES, p. 184.

[14] CES, p. 184.

[15] CES, pp. 184–185.

[16] For his comments about this see Jürgen Habermas, 'A Philosophico-Political Profile', *New Left Review*, **151**, 1985, pp. 75–105.

[17] People only become natives and their actions only turn into behaviour when they are viewed as pure objects from the perspective of an unphilosophically reflective empiricist anthropology that Habermas addresses explicitly in RRS.

[18] Raul Pertierra, 'Forms of Rationality? Rationalization and Social Transformation in a Northern Philippine Community', *Social Analysis*, **17**, August 1985.

[19] See Michael Schmid's 'Habermas' Theory of Social Evolution' in J. Thompson and D. Held (eds), *Habermas: Critical Debates*, Macmillan, London, 1982.

[20] L. Kohlberg, 'Stage and Sequence', in D. Goslin (ed.), *Handbook of Socialization Theory and Research*, Chicago, 1969; also 'From Is to Ought' in T. Mischel (ed.), *Cognitive Development and Epistemology*, New York, 1971, pp. 151–236.

[21] The most concise formulation of Habermas's incorporation of psychological theories is to be found in Ch. 2, 'Moral Development and Ego Identity' of his *Communication and the Evolution of Society*. (CES).

[22] CES, p. 89.

[23] Erik Erikson, *Identity Youth and Crisis,* W. W. Norton, New York, 1968, see especially Ch. 3, 'The Life Cycle: Epigenesis of Identity'; also *Childhood and Society,* New York, 1963, and Ch. 3 of *Identity and The Life Cycle*, New York, 1959.

[24] J. Piaget, *The Moral Judgement of the Child,* New York, 1965, and *Biology and Knowledge,* Chicago, 1971.

[25] See 'Of Gods and Demons: Habermas and Practical Reason', that appears as Ch. 7 in *Habermas: Critical Debates*, J. Thompson and D. Held (eds), Macmillan, London, 1982, esp. p. 146.

[26] For an accessible entry to these discussions see Habermas, *Towards a Rational Society*, Heinemann, London, 1971, Ch. 6, 'Technology and Science as Ideology'.

[27] A paraphrase of his definition of reconstruction given on p. 95 of CES.

[28] Friedrich H. Tenbuck, 'The Problem of Thematic Unity in the Works of Max Weber', *British Journal of Sociology*, **31**, 3, 1980.

[29] See Table 2, Ch. 1.

[30] The quote is from Weber's, *Economy and Society*, p. 556, and appears in Habermas, RRS, p. 173. The emphasis is mine.

[31] In a recent interview — 'A Philosophico-Political Profile', *New Left Review*, **151**, 1985, pp. 75–105 — Habermas agrees that these criticisms are neglected in his work. He also ventures the interesting disclaimer that, 'I doubt whether such revisions would be forced to tamper with the general correlation of an ethics of conviction, worldly asceticism, and economic behaviour' (p. 87).

[32] This is an especially difficult theme to reconstruct in Weber because the threads are scattered through many different texts and periods of his writing. For an extremely clear exposition see Roger Brubaker, *The Limits of Rationality*, Allen & Unwin, London, 1984, pp. 61–91.

[33] See pp. 236–240 of RRS.

[34] RRS p. 292f.

[35] See p. 242 of RRS.

[36] Max Weber, *The Protestant Ethic and the Spirit of Capitalism*, Allen & Unwin, London, 1976, p. 181. The emphasis is mine.

[37] The quote is from Weber's *Economy and Society,* p. 1394, and it appears in Habermas' RRS p. 218. The emphasis is mine.

[38] Weber's *Economy and Society,* p. 1394, and Habermas RRS p. 218. The emphasis is mine.

[39] Weber, *The Protestant Ethic*, p. 183.

[40] RRS, p. 218.

[41] We are reminded here of Weber's remarks first at the beginning of the *Protestant Ethic*, and then in the last paragraph, that 'it is not my aim to substitute for a one-sided materialistic an equally one-sided spiritualistic casual interpretation of culture and history. Each is equally possible, but each, if it does not serve as the preparation, but as the conclusion of an investigation, accomplishes equally little in the interests of historical truth' (p. 183). This is very much Habermas's own position which he works out in his brilliant discussion of 'ideas and interests' in RRS, pp. 187–194 — see especially p. 235.

[42] Especially in his 'Reconstruction of Historical Materialism', CES, Ch. 4, to which I refer the reader with the confession that I find it almost completely impenetrable.

[43] For an interesting and accessible historical sociological discussion of the State that deals with Habermas and is cast in terms of the development of the law, see Gianfranco Poggi, *The Development of the Modern State: A Sociological Introduction*, Stanford University Press, 1978.

[44] Sisters are not excluded and the term 'brotherhood' is used because he is commenting on Weber's original usage.

[45] Skjervheim quoted by Habermas, RRS, p. 112.

[46] 'The Dialectics of Rationalisation: An Interview with Jürgen Habermas', Axel Honneth *et al.*, *Telos*, **49**, pp. 4–31.

[47] RRS, p. 71.

[48] RRS, pp. 71–72.

[49] RRS, p. 135.

[50] If we find the shift from the individual to the collective subject somewhat disconcerting this should only serve to remind us again that in this German tradition it is, by contrast with our own, natural to think of the subject of action first of all in collective terms.

[51] 'A Review of Gadamer's Truth and Method', Jürgen Habermas, in *Understanding and Social Inquiry*, F. R. Dallmayr and T. A. McCarthy (eds.), Notre Dame University Press, 1977, p. 343.

[52] *Ibid.*, p. 432.

[53] RRS, p. 132.

[54] RRS, p. 132.

[55] Paul Ricoeur, 'Habermas and Gadamer in Dialogue', *Philosophy Today*, **17**, 2/4, Summer 1973, pp. 153–165.

[56] *Ibid.*

[57] H. G. Gadamer, 'On the Scope and Function of Hermeneutic Reflection', *Continuum*, **8**, 8, 1970.

[58] Habermas, 'A Review of Gadamer's Truth and Method', in F. R. Dallmayr and T. A. McCarthy, *op. cit.*, p. 360.

[59] *Ibid.*, p. 360.

[60] *Ibid.*, p. 358.

3

Communication and social action

INTRODUCTION

The most ambitious and original feature of Habermas's whole work is his attempt to recast the study of society in a theory of communication. In retrospect it is clear this has been his guiding intention even from his first philosphical statement of the theses for *Knowledge and Human Interests*. In his 1965 inaugural lecture he says [1]:

> What raises us out of nature is the only thing whose nature we can know: language. Through its structure, autonomy and responsibility are posited for us. Our first sentence expresses unequivocally the intention of universal and unconstrained consensus.

Now, some twenty years later, Habermas offers a systematic and explicitly sociological casting of all his major preoccupations — with rationality, social action, and social reproduction — within his 'paradigm of communication'. Through all its shifts and turns and endless reconstructions and debates this enormous project follows a clear and remarkably consistent course.

'SYSTEMATICALLY DISTORTED COMMUNICATION' AND 'IDEAL SPEECH SITUATION'

In this section I shall take some short-cuts through a maze of complexites and try, as simply as possible, to outline the early foundations of Habermas's theory of communicative competence and of communicative action. None of this will make any sense unless Habermas's single aim is kept clearly in mind. He wants to devlop a model that will show how rationality (and irrationality) are manifest in ordinary social interaction, that is to say in ordinary communication between 'speaking and acting subjects'.

How is rationality alternatively made manifest or repressed in ordinary speaking interactions? Where on earth should we look for the more specific forms of speech and action that could guide this otherwise impossibly abstract and useless philosophical search towards sociological realities? In *Knowledge and Human Interests* [2] and then in an enormously influential early article called 'systematically distorted communication' [3] Habermas looks to his philosophical sources, to hermeneutics, to other theories of language and, most importantly in this context, to Freud and to the psychoanalytic relationship between analyst and patient, for the vital constituents of his model. The therapeutic relationship is admittedly no ordinary relationship. Indeed, it is a specialized type of communication; and yet it is carried on in and through ordinary language and conducted in a way that points to *universal characteristics and potentialities of ordinary communication* among speaking and acting subjects. When it succeeds, the psychoanalytic relationship does create for the patient a new freedom. As insight and reflection are brought to bear on hiterto repressed experience the patient achieves a new-found autonomy — an emancipation — and an enlarged measure of *rational control* over his or her actions and interactions. There is the key!

The treatment of Freud (not a good pun) is another excellent example of Habermas's extremely selective use of his classical authors. He simply takes what he wants and incorporates it into his own context in ways that may sometimes completely override the larger intentions of the original author [4]. In this case he has not the slightest interest in Freud's theory of instincts, in the theory of sexuality or, indeed, in any other aspect of Freud's very positivistic social biology. The inspiration comes purely from the *process and method of the therapeutic relationship*. In this relationship we find the source of several of the seminal elements of the later theory of communicative competence and of communicative action.

In the first place, the psychoanalytic relationship demonstrates, fairly concretely, what is achieved through *reflection*. In the security of the therapeutic relationship the therapist deliberately holds back his or her own responses and minimizes all other external pressures in a controlled situation. In this way the patient is able to freely associate conscious thoughts and dreams with repressed or forgotten experience. In short, the patient learns to *reflect* on his or her own experience and in this way to reassimilate repressed material into consciousness and, at the method's best, to *affirm a larger rational control* over complexes of 'sytematically distorted' perceptions, responses, compulsions and inhibitions that lie at the root of the neurosis. In short, reflection is the social process through which irrationally impaired or broken communication is restored and so 'rationally redeemed'.

Second, the process of reflection rationally redeems this 'inner foreign territory' of the perverse Unconscious through the medium of *speech and symbolic interaction*. Hiterto unrecognized disturbances are first identified, discussed, lost and seen again and again, from different points of view. This is always achieved through ordinary processes of naming, suggestion, association, categorization, review, definition and recognition. It is in this way that unconscious and perverse compulsions surrender to the power of language and speech [5].

> An isolated symbolic content . . . strikes us as being a symptom because it has gained private linguistic significance and can no longer be used according to the rules of public language . . . [and cure is effected through] . . . resymbolisation, that is, the re-entry of isolated symbolic contents into public communication.

It is through the process of verbalization that subterranean irrationalities and compulsions are assimilated into a symbolic order that owes its power to the very fact that it is *public*. Even in the relationship between only these two people — patient and therapist — we see that the process of recovery is already a movement towards a *public* world in which unrecognized, repressed, and privatized experience is made cummunicable or, as Habermas will later say, 'discursively redeemed'. As it is shared it is connected with the vast stock of meanings and interpretations that are available only in and through speech and (symbolic) interaction. To corroborate these insights in another way, one need only consider why it is that solitary confinement leads, eventually, to insanity — sanity is of course a social achievement or, as Habermas would say, 'a communicative accomplishment'.

Third, the psychoanalytic relationship also points to the distinctive requirement of a *critical* hermeneutic, and beyond this to a *critical* theory [6]. Critical reflection goes further than hermeneutic understanding because it confronts unconscious complexes that do *not* obediently fall into the widening compass of a hermeneutic circle of interpretation. Some of these systematic distortions can only be unlocked with *explanation,* that is to say with analyses that lead insight to objective events and causes, that have structured the patient's life-history 'from the outside in', and that are now apprehended through social interaction but from an 'externalist perspective', and with the help of critical social scientific theory and knowledge. Systematic distortions are not like misunderstood or unrecognized meanings. They have to be explained. Once our view of the psychoanalytic process is corrected with this insight, we see that its method simultaneously unites and deploys *both* explanation *and* interpretation. More importantly we see that explanation and understanding are both universal potentialities also of ordinary communication and social action.

Fourth, this protean form of critical theory that is built into the psychoanalytic process implicitly employs a model of *deviant socialization*. Systematic distortions of identity and self-understanding are the result of traumas and repressions that always have a *social* origin. If my compulsions and other guilt-induced irrationalities issue from the crushing pressures of introjected social and moral norms in my superego, then there must be something wrong with the whole pattern of social relations in which I was formed. This does not exempt me from responsibility for my own life. The point is rather that *systematically distorted communication points back to systematically distorted social structures,* and so to the effects of power on individual life-histories. Moreover, we see too that the structure of repression in both the individual life and the society unavoidably draws our attention to the silent referents of a larger rationality in *a priori* intimations of truth, freedom, and justice that constantly guide the critical process. Systematically distorted communication points in this way to the very realities it negates (the Hegelian dialectic again) and it unavoidably deploys *a priori* categories (Habermas's Kantian thread).

Fifth, the patient's neurosis is directly manifest in aberrant forms of speech and language usage. The classical symptoms of repression, displacement, repressed identifications, and projection show up through what we might call communicative *in*competences. Communication is systematically distorted because the patient does not properly differentiate between subjective, inter-subjective, and objective orders of reality, or between his or her own self (I), another ego (You), and the impersonal objective world (It). Here already we see the first steps in Habermas's transposition of these three basic categories into the paradigm of communication.

With these several considerations in mind we are better able to grasp two key notions that are central to Habermas's project. One is the notion of the '*ideal speech situation*', and the other is his concept of '*communicative competence*'. Both are closely intertwined.

Obviously Habermas has no interest in the particular contents and categories of this or that neurosis. The systematically distorted *form* of neurotically imparied communication is interesting because it holds a key to normal communication and beyond this to the ideal speech situation. Although the relationship between analyst and analysand is a specialized relationship it still contains, in its form, a situation that is always potentially possible in ordinary interactions between speaking and acting subjects [7].

No matter how the intersubjectivity of mutual understanding may be deformed, the *design* of an ideal speech situation is necessarily implied in the structure of potential speech, since all speech, even of intentional deception, is oriented towards the idea of truth.

What Habermas is trying to capture for his model is the formal ideal of a *situation* in which disagreements and conflicts are rationally resolved through a mode of communication which is completely free of compulsion and in which only the force of the better argument may prevail. Again the therapeutic relationship has helped furnish some clearer specifications of what this could mean. Its most instructive feature is that it operates simultaneously on two levels of communication. At the mundane level the patient is merely helped to put his or her thoughts, dreams, and experiences into words. However, the distinctive feature of the psychoanalytic situation is that the patient can at any moment use the relationship to take a *critical* perspective — or, better, a critically *reflective* perspective — on his or her own material. Indeed this is the condition for success and the only way of dissolving the compulsions, of closing the 'gaps' in the semantic field, and of correcting the systematic distortions. The therapist is there to help the patient 'institutionalize' in their relationship a fluent communication about his or her own communications. In this way, therapy deliberately restores and mobilizes a function of ordinary communication. It shows again that, 'ordinary language permits communication only on condition that it is *simultaneously* metacommunication' [8].

In an early article Habermas explains that . . . communicative competence does mean the mastery of the means of construction necessary for the establishment of an ideal-speech situation [9]. And so with this notion of communicative competence Habermas refers to the several means of using language to create consensus and agreement between two or more speaking and acting subjects. Our attention is directed beyond the syntactical and grammatical rules of this or that (English or French) language to the universal means in which *speech* is used to create and sustain *social relationships*. In a sense we are talking about universal skills of communication. We are born with the potential to use them to create a better society.

Mere linguistic competence simply presupposes that speaking and acting subjects have an adequate vocabulary and the grammatical skills necessary to produce well-formed sentences. To constitute and then carry on a dialogue we must be able to use language in a way that differentiates between subjective, inter-subjective, and objective domains of reference — the three fundamental catagories tranposed into three different relations to the world. Moreover, since conflict and disagreement and a certain natural variability of experience are part of the human condition, you and I must both know how to recognize, and to bracket, whatever comes into contention between us. We must be able to resolve disagreements through another kind of dialogue that is carried on at the critically reflective level in what Habermas calls a 'discourse' — this is his term for that special form of interaction in which we suspend action so as to mutually question our basic assumptions and commitments [10]. This will be articulated more precisely and systematically as we follow Habermas's next steps in the following sections: all that needs to be stressed here is that these competencies are manifest, however imperfectly, in ordinary social interaction between ordinary people. There is no need to associate these competencies with the specialized work of 'intellectuals': they are formal constructions of *universal* aspects of speech, or, if one finds the term useful, 'dialogue-constitutive universals' [11].

The basic aims and intentions of these early writings are pursued in the later more developed work with different means, and in the light of criticisms that Habermas has drawn in the many debates that he has willingly entered over the last decade and a half. Two criticisms are especially important because Habermas has accepted them and accordingly changed the mould of his work in order better to deal with them.

In the first place, the psychoanalytic relationship between patient and therapist is a special kind of formally structured relationship that is in most respects not directly analogous with ordinary social relations. Despite Habermas's attempts to deal with the difficulties [12] there is no escape from the problem that 'the revolutionary struggle is by no means a psychoanalytic treatment on a large scale'. The authority of the doctor is voluntarily accepted by the patient for the sake of the cure, whereas, in the larger social context, 'resistance is the common presupposition of all' [13].

A second problem arises because all these early formulations are still too strongly rooted in the philosophy of consciousness and tied to the image of a single speaker or hearer. Even though the image is, at least in Habermas's intentions, always generalized to include a speech- community it is still of limited sociological significance because, as his friend Richard Bernstein remarks, it is insufficiently dialogical [14].

> One primary reason — perhaps the primary reason — for the 'linguistic turn is that it no longer entraps us in the *monological* perspective of a philosophy of the subject. Communicative action

is intrinscially *dialogical*. The starting point for an analysis of the pragmatics of speech is the situation of a speaker and a hearer who are oriented to *mutual* reciprocal understanding; a speaker and hearer who have the capacity to take an affirmative or negative stance when a validity claim is challenged.

SPEECH–ACTIONS

These early writings were first approximations. They point reliably towards the goal of developing a critical social theory that puts rationality and communication at its centre. Yet it is only when we pause to consider what such a mighty project entails that we see how much more has yet to be done. All the basic building blocks of sociology have to be shifted into the paradigm of communication. This charges Habermas with an onus to meet some very exacting requirements. Every sociology contains notions of culture and knowledge. Accordingly, Habermas has to show us how culture and knowledge can be advantageously transposed into the relational terms of a communications model. The gates, once opened, invite other equally fundamental questions. How shall we represent the socialization process in communicative terms? How shall we transpose regulative legal and social norms into a communications paradigm? How can the reproduction of society, from one generation to the next, be conceived as a 'communicative achievement'?

In order to break new ground and to avoid sabotaging his own project, Habermas must, on one side, avoid all regressions into the philosophy of consciousness. On the other hand, his model of social action must guard against all tendencies to scientize society into a thing-like entity that would again subsume all action under a false empiricism of cause and behaviour. And the whole project has to be carried off in a way that will rescue Weber and Marx (and also Durkheim, Parsons, and Mead) from their own 'mistakes', as it explains, more clearly than before, how late capitalist society has developed 'one-sidedly' and in a way that selectively favours the institutionalization of only instrumental and rational purposive-structures of action.

In what is to follow I want to outline the three major thrusts of this transposition into the paradigm of communication. The first is developed under the rubric of a 'universal pragmatics' and the second under the terms of communicative versus strategic action. The third is the model of the lifeworld and system that we have already introduced.

Habermas's attempts to recast social theory into a more concrete model of language usage in ordinary social interaction, as we saw, very soon exhaust the resources of hermeneutics and of other aspects of his German (*Geisteswissenschaften*) tradition. Habermas's ingenuity and the sheer breadth of his erudition ensure that he will always find his resources somewhere, and often in unexpected places. This time his search for sharper tools and categories takes him to one green oasis in the desert of modern British and American analytic philosophy [15], more specifically to the post-Wittgensteinian 'ordinary language philosophy' [16] of Austin, Searle, and Strawson.

Again it is the purpose of the search that points to the value of the find. In this literature Habermas finds a clear break with the (positivistic) reduction of all truth claims to descriptive statements and formal propositions. For Wittgenstein, truth claims arise in language games that are inseparably bound up with 'forms of life'. In other words, they have a *social context!* That is the opening Habermas wants. In the subsequent post-Wittgensteinian ordinary language philosophy there are further developments that Habermas is quick to take over into his own framework — with the same single-minded selectivity with which he approached Freud and all his other texts.

It is Austin and Searle who develop a theory of speech-*acts*. From Habermas's point of view this is a wonderful innovation: here we have a *synthesis of language and action* in a theory of speech-*actions*. And this minor revolt against the empricist orthodoxies offers up some other assistance in the person of Peter Strawson and his 'performative theory of truth' that is tellingly aimed against the 'correspondence theory of truth' — according to which true statements corrrespond, in some atomistic way, with objective factors 'out there'. With Austin and Searle, Strawson turns statements into (social) 'performances': 'Facts are what statements (when true) state; they are not, like things or events on the face of the globe, witnessed or heard or seen, broken or overturned, interrupted or prolonged, kicked, destroyed, mended or noisy' [17]. And so truth is understood anew as an aspect of action, as something that acting subjects *do* — in English, at Oxford and Cambridge, and certainly elsewhere as well!

Habermas has taken over and re-worked Austin's very important distinction between locutionary and illocutionary speech-acts. In Habermas's version this leads first to a twofold, and then to a threefold, distinction of different types of validity claims that are typically raised in ordinary speech actions. In the first place, (locutionary or constative) speech-acts typically proffer statements about an object. This is the dimension of speech-actions in which speakers (and hearers) use language *cognitively* to affirm (and accept) statements with *propositional* content. It corresponds with the first of the *three basic orientations to the world* that speakers and hearers take up in communicative interaction. A simple example would be, 'It's warming up; the snow's melting'. Ordinary scientific argument and discourse is grounded in just this form. There is a clear objective reference to something in the external world that is offered for assessment as true or not true.

What is somewhat less obvious, but equally important, is the further consideration that [18]:

> Truth is merely the most conspicuous — not the only — validity claim reflected in the formal structures of speech. The illocutionary force of the speech act, which produces a legitimate (or illegitimate) interpersonal relation between the participants, is borrowed from the binding force of recognised norms of action (or evaluation); to the extent that a speech act is an action, it actualises an already-established pattern of relations.

Habermas is pointing here, with Austin and Searle, to a second type of validity claim that is raised with the illocutionary or performative dimension of a speech-act. The point is that the speech-action (above) contains another element that is only made explicit when a usually unstated element is added thus: '[I hereby assure you that] it's warming up and that the snow is melting'. It contains a 'promise', an assurance, that is to say, an *illocutionary* component that leads us with Austin to consider [19]:

> If then we loosen up our ideas of truth and falsity we shall see that statements, when assessed in relation to facts, are not so different after all from pieces of advice, warnings, verdicts, and so on . . . [and] . . . We see that, when we have an order or a warning or a piece of advice, there is a question that arises when we discuss how a statement is related to fact.

Our attention is directed accordingly to the *interactive use of language* and to the vast array to tacit warnings, guarantees, admonitions, cautions, recommendations, and promises, and the like, that are just as must part of ordinary speech as the propositions proffered in the *cognitive use of language*. These elements orient speaker and hearer to inter-subjectively recognized *norms* of social action that we may or may not accept; in short, they raise the validity claim of normative rightness and correspond with the second of Habermas's basic orientations (or 'world relations') of speakers and hearers in communicative interaction. Just as the cognitive use of language oriented speaker and hearer to the representation of facts in an external world of natural phenomena, so also, in a parallel way, the interactive use of language orients speaker and hearer to the establishment of legitimate interpersonal relations in 'our' inter-subjectively shared world of society.

In the cognitive use of language a speaker and hearer may not choose explicitly to bring normative validity claims into question. Conversely, of course, an interaction that focuses explicitly on the legitimacy of this or that norm may not involve any explicit reference to external facts. Yet both types of claim are *internally connected in the very constitution of ordinary language communcation*. In this sense both are simultaneously joined in the typical speech-actions of (adult) speakers with a minimum of communicative competence.

Relations between communicatively competent speakers and hearers deploy another function of speech that is built into ordinary language use in exactly the same way. In the expressive use of language, every typical speech action carries the voiced or silent guarantee of the *sincerity* or truthfulness with which I, the speaker, am expressing my inner feelings, needs, and intentions to you, the hearer. It is in that dimension that speech orients you, the hearer, to 'my' inner world of feelings and motives, and so to an assessment of the *authenticity* (or inauthenticity) of what I say. Even when someone is talking to me quite formally about a scientific project, or a cost estimate for an extension to my house, I am, as a communicatively competent adult, still listening for evidence of the truthfulness and sincerity of the speaker. This of course corresponds with the third of these basic orientations of communicatively interacting speakers and hearers.

With these distinctions and categories in mind we have the rudiments of what Habermas presents as the *universal* pragmatic features of speech-actions and hence also of *communicative competence*. The schema can be simplified as shown in Table 3 [20].

COMMUNICATIVE ACTION

Those who have survived a brutally over-simplified journey through these abstractions will be heartened to discover that they have long since passed into the theory of communicative action. In considering speech-actions we have, of course, been assembling the building blocks of communicative action. The other constituents are assembled, as we have noted, from the reconstructions of Weber and Marx, and also of Parsons, Mead, Durkheim, Lukács, Adorno, Horkheimer and others. Since there is no possibility of dealing comprehensively with the complexities of 1200 pages of abstract arguments I shall use the foregoing discussions as a background against which, first, to bring the notion of communicative action into a clearer focus, and then, secondly, to point, with some very brief and

Table 3

Mode of communication	Cognitive	Interactive	Expressive
Type of speech-actions	Constatives	Regulatives	Avowals
Domains of reality	'The' world of external nature	'Our' world of society	'My' world of internal nature
Basic attitude	Objectivating	Norm-conformative	Expressive
General functions of speech	Representation of facts	Establishment of legitimate interpersonal relations	Disclosure of speaker's subjectivity
Validity claim	Truth	(Normative) rightness	Truthfulness (sincerity)

selective comments, to three central thrusts of the theory — with respect (a) to liberal and utilitarian theories of rationality, action and society, (b) to Weber's theory of the rationalization process, and (c) to social reproduction.

The theory of communicative action shifts the fulcrum of social theory into the now *fully dialogical* and quintessentially *social* relationship of two or more speakers and hearers who, reciprocally and simultaneously, proffer not one kind of validity claim but three. This is the core of Habermas's innovation. Communicative interaction is the medium through which speaking and acting subjects interlace their speech-action. It is through this medium and through the ordinary process of 'reaching an understanding' [*Verständigung*] that we are bound together — for the most part gently and imperceptibly — by the rationally motivating force of our mundane agreements and communicatively formed convictions. Habermas formally reconstructs this process in the following terms [21]:

> When a hearer accepts a speech act, an agreement [*Einverständnis*] comes about between at least two acting and speaking subjects . . . an agreement of this sort is achieved simultaneously at three levels . . . . As the medium for achieving understanding,

speech acts serve: (1) to establish and renew interpersonal relations, whereby the speaker takes up a relation to something in the
world of legitimate (social) orders; (b) to represent (or presuppose) states and events, whereby the speaker takes up a
relation to something in the world of existing states of affairs; (c)
to manifest experiences — that is to represent oneself — whereby
the speaker takes up a relationship to something in the subjective
world to which he has privileged access. Communicatively
achieved agreement is measured against exactly three criticizable
validity claims; in coming to an understanding about something
with one another and thus making themselves understandable,
actors cannot avoid embedding their speech acts in precisely three
world-relations and claiming validity for them under these
aspects.

With the benefit of this context, Habermas's notion of 'communicative
rationality' is no longer nearly so mysterious. We can now, in his words, use
it 'without blushing' because it is clear that it refers to the three dimensions
in which speaking and acting subjects reciprocally proffer three different
types of claims for each others' agreement in communicative interaction.
All three dimensions are built into the very structure of speech communication. In this threefold structure of communicative interaction we find the
social core of our species nature — and the central point of the 'lingusitic
turn' of Habermas's mature work. Accordingly, it must be the case that the
'original mode' [22] of communication, the archetypal form of communication, the paradigmatic form of communication, and certainly the most
comprehensively rational form of communication (choose your own way of
stressing the point) must be *action that is oriented to reaching an understanding across all three dimensions*. And that indeed is what communicative action means.

It is in just these terms that Habermas counterposes 'action oriented to
reaching and understanding' with 'action that is oriented to success'.

(1) With the theory of communicative action it has been Habermas's
aim to overturn the monological individualism of liberal and utilitarian
theories of society. He has tried, once and for all, to lift social theory clear
of pseudo-sociological generalizations of society based on the model of a
single individual oriented to the world solely in terms of his or her own
strategic calculations (of the relative cost and benefits of this or that action.)
These theories can offer no plausible account of how identity is socially
constructed or of how actions are socially coordinated. All these problems
are usually implausibly explained with a 'sticks 'n' carrots' theory of

Action situation \ Action orientation	Oriented to success	Oriented to reaching under-standing
Nonsocial	instrumental action	– – – – –
Social	strategic action	communicative action

Fig. 4 — Types of action [23].

sanctions, roles and motivations that mystifies the very social processes that it seeks to illuminate. The implicit model of rationality is still more fundamentally defective.

In Fig. 4 *instrumental (zweckrational) action* has its place. And yet, in so far as it is oriented only to success through the technological control of impersonal problems, it does not even count as social action because it is not really communicatively mediated [24]. On the other hand, *strategic actions* are instrumental actions oriented towards success over a rational opponent with competing interests. It is here that we immediately recognize the form of action that has central place in the competitive individualism of liberal and utilitarian theories of society. In the face of some criticism Habermas insists that strategic action is not just an analytic term and that stategic actions are real social actions that are clearly distinguishable from communicative action in that they are coordinated through interest positions.

With these distinctions and the several difficult arguments in which they are set, Habermas seeks to show that all goal-directed actions oriented towards success are, necessarily and unavoidably, socially coordinated through the medium of language — in short, they are linguistically mediated. When goal-directed and strategic actions are seen in this context and against the broader potentialities for rational action that are given in the very structures of language communication, we are better able to grasp the partiality — the 'one-sidedness' of the model of rationality and action with which they are usually justified and defended. Rationality reckoned in this narrow way is coordinated only in one single dimension: it suppresses the possibility of making actions maximally rational by cordinating them socially, through the medium of language, in the two other dimensions in which the 'generalizable interests' of the interacting persons are always tacitly proffered — and in this case repressed and ignored. It is against this more comprehensive standard of rationality — namely of communicative rationality — that Habermas turns the tables against utilitarians and liberal theories and assigns strategic action to its properly subordinate place in the critical theory of society.

(2) Weber's image of modernity as an historically inevitable imprisonment within the Iron Cage of late capitalism must be corrected because it has a burning contemporary relevance that is mistakenly grounded, again, in a one-sided model of rationality. Weber's prescient vision of our modern condition is in fact a one-sided selection from an open set of possibilities. The inherent bias has to be rectified with corrections to the one-sided model of rationality on which it is based.

To Weber's 'official typology of action' [25] Habermas counterposes an alternative typology (Fig. 5). With the category of '*de facto* customary

Degree of rationality action Coordination	Low	High
Through interest position	*de facto* customary action [*Sitte*]	strategic action [*Interessenhandeln*]
Through normative agreement	conventional action based on agreement [*Gemeinschaftshandeln*]	post-conventional action based on agreement [*Gesellschaftshandeln*]

Fig. 5 — An alternative typology of action [26]

action' Habermas has in mind the kind of half-conscious and comparatively simple reckoning of group and family interests that coordinates social action in the relatively settled situation that one might — perhaps with too much historical and anthropological naivety — typically associated with pre-modern social formations. Depsite the many difficulties posed by these comparisons [27], sociocultural rationalization certainly does correspond with a quantum leap in the degree of formal rationality and so with greatly expanded possibilities for the strategic coordination of actions — through the ever-more-refined calculations of interest that are made possible by the information technologies and organizational structures of modern capitalism. No one can say that tax lawyers, market researchers, policy analysts and computer-linked futures exchanges are not extremely highly rationalized means of calculating and coordinating the stragetic interests of those who use them.

Weber's vision of modernity is so one-sided because rationalization is, as we have seen, conceived mainly, if not exclusively, in these terms and leads accordingly to the 'Iron Cage' (to 'rationalization as the loss of freedom' and 'rationalization as the loss of meaning'). What Habermas wants to show is that, as the customs of traditional society break up, their normative and value-rational elements are *not necessarily* destined, as Weber supposed, to vanish altogether or else to remain *only* in the form of mere conventions psychologically enforced only through a mixture of habit and sanctions. What *is* inevitable is that the process of modernization will dissolve the traditional customs, but, beyond this, it is by no means inevitable that it should slip into the 'one-sided' course of the rationalization *only* of rational–purposive structures of action. Weber's 'mistake' is that he does not see that higher levels of rationalization, strategically accomplished through the coordination of complementary interests, *does not necessarily preclude the much broader possibility of also rationalizing action in the 'post-conventional' form of communicatively achieved agreement — across all three dimensions of communicative action.*

In the history of modern Europe, Weber discerns an increasingly differentiated institutionalization of science, morals, and art. It is this threefold differentiation at the level of institutional structures that has inspired Habermas to press the reconstructions of Weber through to completion in a way that clears the bottlenecks of his monological theory of action and carries the whole threefold scheme into a theory of communicative action. The world-historical process of rationalization reconstructed anew along these lines dispels the misconceived inevitability of the 'Iron Cage'. It represents *one* view of modernity that is now put in its perspective, as a 'one-sided selection' from among alternatives that also include the possibility of society built on a more comprehensively rational application of communicative rationality to the problems of the human condition.

(3) Communicative action and the reproduction of society: as we have seen: 'Processes of reaching an understanding aim at an agreement that meets the conditions of rationally motivated assent [*Zustimmung*] to the content of an utterance. A communicative achievement has a rational basis . . . [it] rests on common convictions' [28]. It is against the background of Weber's threefold scheme and with the help of a theory of speech-actions that Habermas seeks to spell out what he intends with his insistence that, 'reaching understanding is the inherent *telos* of human speech' [29]. However, he quickly orders a stop to any trivializing reduction of communicative action to purely linguistic analyses of the chatter of speech-acts at the surface of social interaction. He insists that:

'Communicative action is *not exhausted* by the act of reaching understanding in an interpretative manner . . . communicative action designates a type of interaction that is *co-ordinated through* speech-acts and does *not co-incide with* them [30]. In other words, there is something more: 'Every process of reaching understanding takes place against the background of a culturally ingrained pre-understanding' [31]. Whatever is proffered or made explicit in communicative action is, as we have seen, drawn up from our shared *lifeworld* — from a lifeworld that is always 'holistically structured' and only partially amenable to consciousness because it is ever 'behind our backs'. The fuller sociological ramifications of the theory are all missed unless we see that it is not just this or that particular speech-action that is shared in communicative action. If we may borrow Plato's metaphor and look from the small letters to the large letters we see that communicative action is another way of pointing to *the communicative reproduction of society* [32]:

> it is only with the turn back to the context-forming horizon of the lifeworld, from within which participants in communication come to an understanding with one another about something, that our field of vision changes in such a way that we can see the points of connection for social theory within the theory of communicative action: The concept of society has to be linked to a concept of the lifeworld that is complementary to the concept of communicative action. Then communicative action becomes interesting primarily as a principle of sociation.

These insights redirect attention to the evolution of society, and more specifically to the unevenness of the rationalization process. The modernization process releases an expanding potential for communicatively achieved agreement. As Habermas explains with his reconstructions of Durkheim and Mead, the ritually enforced and sacred social forms and practices of earlier societies are gradually secularized, and thus 'liquefied', and opened to progressively more conscious communicative interaction and possible change. In this proess we do not 'discover' any kind of ontogically given Reason — with a capital 'R' — that is somehow built into history and society. That was always an idealist fantasy. Instead we are forced to rely on our own shared, and quintessentially social, capacity for communication and understanding. As we have seen with the 'linguistic turn' of his mature work Habermas has sought to articulate the three-dimensional form of this capacity for communication and understanding that is our ultimate resource.

Yet this potential for communicatively achieved agreement is blocked, at the social-structural level, by the exploitative organizational principle of capitalism and hence converted to forms that are geared to the partial interests of the powerful few. In short, the communicative reproduction of society is, as we shall see, selectively steered into the 'one-sided' pattern of late capitalism through the media of power and money.

NOTES

[1] KHI, p. 314.

[2] See especially KHI, Ch. 10, 'Self-Reflection as Science: Freud's Psychoanalytic Critique of Meaning'.

[3] 'Systematically Distorted Communication', *Inquiry*, **13,** 1970.

[4] Harbermas is perfectly aware of the criticism that this sometimes evokes. He admits 'Even when I quote a good deal and take over other terminologies I am clearly aware that my use of them often has little to do with the author's original meaning'; p. 30 of 'The Dialectics of Rationalisation; An interview with Jürgen Habermas', by Axel Honneth *et al., Telos,* **49,** pp. 5–31.

[5] 'Systematically Distorted Communication', see note [3].

[6] See the section 'Method and meaning' of Chapter 2.

[7] p. 372, 'Towards a Theory of Communicative Competence', *Inquiry,* **13,** 1970, pp. 360–375.

[8] 'A Postscript to Knowledge and Human Interests', *Philosophy of the Social Sciences,* 1973, pp. 157–189.

[9] 'Towards a Theory of Communicative Competence', p. 372, (see note [7]).

[10] The mutual obiligation to create this situation — in which only the force of the better argument may prevail — is covered by what Habermas calls 'communicative ethics'.

[11] The term is used in 'Towards a Theory of Communicative Competence', (see note [7]).

[12] See especially the Introduction to *Theory and Practice,* trans. John Viertel, Heinemann, London, 1974, esp. pp. 28–32.

[13] The criticisms are offered by G. H. Gadamer and J. J. Giegel and represented by Habermas on pp. 29–32 of his *Theory and Practice* (see note [12]).

[14] p. 18 of Bernstein's excellent critical introduction to Habermas in *Habermas and Modernity,* edited by Richard J. Bernstein, Polity Press, 1985.

[15] It is Habermas who sees it as a desert! — "By scientism I mean the basic orientation prevailing in analytic philsophy", Postscript to Knowledge and Human Interests, *Phil Soc. Sci.,* 1973, p. 158. — That I should agree is of no particular consequence.

[16] For an excellent sample see, *Philosophy and Ordinary Language,* Charles E. Caton (ed.), University of Illinois Press, 1963.

[17] P. F. Stawson, 'Truth', in G. Pitcher (ed.), *Truth,* Prentice-Hall, Englewood Cliffs, NJ, 1964, p. 38; quoted thus by Habermas in 'A Postscript to Knowledge and Human Interests', *op. cit.,* p. 167.

[18] CES pp. 53–54.In one of several technical qualifications to which I cannot refer here Habermas explains that this applies only to 'propositionally differentiated' speech acts'. For the important details of this first formulation see 'What is a Universal Pragmatics?' that appears as Ch. 1 of CES. For the later version, see esp. pp. 319–337 of RRS.

[19] From J. L. Austin, *Performative Utterances,* pp. 250–251, as quoted by Habermas in CES, p. 55.

[20] In this schema I have, with some simplifications and omissions, collapsed together two of Habermas's tables that appear on pp. 58 and 68 of CES, respectively.

[21] RRS, pp. 307–308.

[22] RRS, p. 288.

[23] RRS, p. 285.

[24] It is in the typical case set in written and technical languages rather than ordinary language in spoken form.

[25] See Chapter 1 p. 000, and Habermas, RRS, p. 282.

[26] RRS, p. 283.

[27] Although there is no space to go into the matter here, it should be noted that to the eye of many social historians and anthropologists this is much more controversial than it seems. Many people would argue, from the perspective of a cultural relativism which is deeply ingrained in modern anthropology, that action in these situations is extremely complex and just as sophisticated as the so-called 'modern' structures of action of our own societies.

[28] RRS, p. 287.

[29] RRS, p. 287.

[30] RRS, p. 101.

[31] RRS, p. 100.

[32] RRS, p. 337.

4

The political sociology of advanced capitalist societies

'The pursuit of happiness' might one day mean something different—for example, not accumulating material objects of which one
disposes privately, but bringing about social relations in which
mutuality predominates and satisfaction does not mean triumph
of one over the repressed needs of the other.[1]

INTRODUCTION

Imagine putting some questions to an English-speaking gathering of fairly
well-educated people with at least some familiarity with the social sciences.
Ask them firstly which of three general complexes of relations—economic,
political, and 'social'—has the strongest part in shaping the daily life of our
'post-industrial' or 'late capitalist' societies. The answers won't be too
ambiguous. They will say that the economy is, of course (!), the strongest
most of the time, then politics, then the 'social', whatever that means, and
we are not at all sure. Then invite them to consider the more unfamiliar
question as to how and in what degree these three complexes of relations
define and set *limits* on each other. After some puzzling the answers may
well be that, yes, obviously the economic system sets limits on political and
social relations— financial, labour and stock markets together with interna-
tional trading positions and the strength of the currency all fix national
income in a way that sets unyielding limits on political and social relations.
And, yes, written or unwritten constitutions and long-established politcal
conventions together with the whole apparatus of the State do have a

substantiality that sets legal, administrative, and other *limits* on the 'social order', which our gathering will probably construe as the family, education, welfare and health care systems and perhaps also 'the class structure'.

In these imagined responses there is a kind of hierarchy of causal efficacy and substantiality. References to 'the economy' call up images of a hard 'nature-like' entity to which political and sociocultural relations must adapt. Political relations seem also to have sharp and hard referents such as parliaments, laws, and bureaucracies that define and limit social action in all kinds of apparently obvious ways.

Once formal public sector organizations such as hospitals, schools, prisons, and child-care centres are more appropriately classified as a part of the State, 'social relations', our third term, either becomes a marxist euphemism for the ensemble of class relations or merely a residual category for a vast array of diffuse social interactions that has, in the normal perspectives of English-speaking social science, practically no substantiality and no sure forms at all! In the light of the preceding chapters we shall not be surprised to find now, in what is to follow, that the original and distinctive feature of Habermas's political sociology is that it challenges these prejudices and seeks to persuade us that the ultimate limits of political contestation and change in advanced capitalist societies are to be found in what has too prematurely been given up as the formless morass of ordinary social interaction. It must be said once again that Habermas does not minimize the political significance of the market nor of established political institutions. As we shall see, his originality lies rather in his elaborately argued view that the sociocultural order has an equal importance and that it is *not* infinitely yielding or plastic—or, to make the same point more positively, that it has a decisive part in shaping the stress lines, crisis tendencies, the 'survival limits' and the dynamics, of advanced capitalist societies. The common thread, from the first philosophical statements through the theory of the evolution of society and the reconstruction of Weber, is always the same. The constitution and dynamic of society is never reducible to its social–structural and economic substratum (as in the marxist version), nor is it reducible to meanings, ideas and cultural forms (as in the idealist, 'culturalist' or hermeneutic version): it is instead a result of an interaction between the two, an interaction in which each dimension conditions and sets *limits* on the other. This is the constant theme that binds together the changing emphases of his twenty years of writings on politics and power. It will be useful to consider Habermas's critical social theory of advanced capitalism in the three stages in which it has appeared.

In the remainder of this introduction I shall comment on aspects of his political sociology that appear before its important reformulation, within a systems framework, in *Legitimation Crisis* and its revisions [2]. The second section discusses the legitimation and motivation crises in relation to the State. Finally, in the third and last section, I want to follow the political sociology through to 'the linguistic turn' of his latest work.

Early formulations

Habermas's *Strukturwandel der Öffentlichkeit* (Structural Transformation of the Public Sphere) was originally published in 1962—some 25 years before its English translation [3]. It offers many insights into the conceptual origins of the political sociology and invites some criticisms that will recur in later phases of the work. To grasp the larger significance of this notion of a 'public sphere' one should try to imagine a society in which there is no politically effective public discussion or voluntary association and the like, 'between' the private family, the market economy, and the formal apparatus of the State (parliaments, bureaucracies, the law, the military, etc.). What would freedom, politics and, indeed, society mean under these conditions and how would that society be integrated?

From the Hegelian and also the French [4] idea of a *civil society* as a plurality of mediating associations between the family and state [5], Habermas builds his own concept of a public sphere. He describes it as follows [6]:

> By the 'public sphere' we mean first of all a realm of our social life in which something approaching public opinion can be formed . . .. Citizens behave as a public body when they confer in an unrestricted fashion—that is, with the guarantee of freedom of assembly and association and the freedom to express and publish their opinions—about matters of general interest . . .. The expression 'public opinion' refers to the tasks of criticism and control which a public body of citizens informally practises . . . *vis-à-vis* a ruling class.

In this concept we find his first attempt to join together informal interaction, communication, and rational discourse [7]. The concept has many affinities with the classical Greek *polis*, and more importantly, with the liberal theory of liberty and democracy of J. S. Mill and others. These connections are by no means accidental since Habermas, like the young Marx, is impressed with the advances in political freedom achieved in eighteenth- and nineteenth-centry France and the high points of British parliamentary government that he dates from 1832 to 1867.

In the pursuit of its own interests, this nineteenth-century bourgeoisie institutionalized open-ended public debate as a necessary condition for the legitimation of political and state action [8]. In these moments, rational debate in a partly autonomous 'public sphere' is institutionalized and thus, as Poggi [9] has explained, there arises a new situation in which the validity of the law no longer rests upon the will of the prince, divine authority, or consanguinity; nor, in Hegel's words, 'upon force, nor primarily upon habits and mores, but upon insights and arguments'. In this public sphere, action is, in principle, legitimated in terms of generalizable interests that transcend the particular interests of competing groups and individuals. In this way the bourgeois public sphere gives some historical specificity and content to what Habermas calls 'rational will formation'. In the same way it gives specificity to the notion, reconstructed from Weber, of practical rationality, for here at last we can begin to see how the ethos and value commitments of large communities of citizens can imbue social action with 'structure-forming effects' in a politically significant way.

Although Habermas never claimed, as some marxists imagine, that the public sphere was independent of property relations, we are still faced with the somewhat embarrassingly brute fact that its modern development historically coincides with the ugliest period of nineteenth century industrial capitalism. Real and massive shifts of power did occur (from the nobility to the new industrial and mercantile bourgeoisie) and these changes may have been driven by rational debate and consensus, but no one doubts that the consensus so achieved included only a relatively small elite who already shared a common cultural, familial, and educational inheritance—marxist critics would point, for example, to the last decades of the nineteenth century in England and there to the pre-existing (and class-bound?) ties among the members of a well-formed Establishment of civil servants, members of parliament, industrialists and bankers and the like [10]. These are some among many of the difficult problems raised by Habermas's very controversial—and some would say altogether inadequate [11]—attempts to ground his concepts in real history.

As the focus moves into our own century and more specifically towards the features of 'late' or advanced capitalism we are faced with the unexpected and puzzling coincidence of mass democracy, affluence, and a degradation of the public sphere. In the middle decades of this century, mass education, increasing social mobility, and in short the whole process of 'modernization and development' brings with it not rationality and emancipation but rather, to Habermas's eye, a deepening *irrationality*. Late capitalism brings with it the manipulation of public opinion through the mass media, the forced articulation of social needs through large organizations, and in short, the management of politics, by 'the system'. A population that is, at last, educated and affluent, as never before seems, paradoxically, to have become the object rather than the subject of politics. Moreover, advanced capitalism in the West gives the lie to the image of a 'class conscious, struggling proletariat' as the bearer of Reason or even as the engine of social change, revolution, or emancipation. At the same time the Soviet Russian experience vindicates Weber's prediction that the abolition of private property, and hence of class relations and structures, would not of itself do anything to relieve political domination and repression. New circumstances demand a revision of classical marxist analyses of capitalism based on strict notions of class and labour and ask for more developed studies of power, ideology, and the State—all underdeveloped concepts in Marx's analysis of an earlier form of liberal capitalist society.

Habermas's several attempts to grapple with the irrational and repressive impact of 'rationalization' and 'development' lead him to examine a new form of ideology. He calls it the 'technocratic consciousness'. There is of course nothing new about the concept of *ideology per se*. Power that serves partial rather than common interests has to be either hidden or legitimated with 'ideas' and with cultural forms that we call ideology. What Habermas does is to point to the new *form* of ideology in late capitalist society. The roots of his analysis are immediately familiar: just as science, learning, and philosophy are perverted in our own time through a one-sided assimilation of ethics and reason into scientific/technological categories so also do we recognize another face of the same phenomenon in the political order. Science and technology fuse together into a new productive force that reappears, not as something that is man/woman-made to serve us according to larger and freely chosen purposes, but rather as an independent variable of 'development'—a notion that is now narrowed to mean only economic development facilitated by a State with no other purpose.

Ideologies in earlier periods of capitalism had a very different character inasmuch as they selected, amplified, and distorted ethically loaded images of the good life. We remember for example how, in the time of the 'Great War', millions of young men were lured to enlist, fight and die for the greater glory of 'God, King, Country and Empire'. And of course French colonialism in the first half of this century was similarly justified with the ideology of *'une mission civilisatrice'* that would so generously bestow all the benefits of French life and culture on the populations of North Africa and Indo-China. By contrast, the distinct feature of ideology in our own society is, according to Habermas, that all 'practical substance' and collective ethical projections are seemingly dissolved [12].

> The technocratic consciousness reflects not the sundering of [particular] ethical situations but the repression of ethics as such as a category of life. The common positivist way of thinking renders inert the frame of reference of interaction in ordinary language . . . as the reified models of the sciences migrate into the

sociocultural life-world and gain objective power over the latter's self-understanding. The ideological nucleus of this consciousness is the elimination of the distinction between the practical and the technical. . . . Technocratic consciousness makes this practical interest disappear behind the interest in the expansion of our power of technical control.

In this transformation of ideology in late capitalist society we recognize the 'political content of science and technology' and the political dimension of the rationalization process as Weber foresaw it in his fateful prospect of the Iron Cage of late capitalism.

These two analyses—of the public sphere and of ideology—are complementary one to the other. The public sphere points to possibilities for genuine, emancipatory, rationalization that are masked and endangered by this new positivistic ideology of the technocratic consciousness. And, in so far as this ideology runs into limits, it points to 'repressed traces of Reason' and to a communicative rationality, that is always ready as a latent 'avenging force' for Reason in history. Both of these early statements are grounded, as Habermas intended, in a new and more adequate philosophical framework. From *Knowledge and Human Interests* through to these first formulations of the political sociology it is clear that Habermas has already worked out, at least in outline, the basic standard against which he will probe, 'measure', and define the irrationality of late capitalism. Even at this early stage the standard is firmly tied to the 'counter-factual' ideal of a reconstructed practical rationality in which reason becomes active in politics and history through the free interpenetration, in unrestricted social interaction, of instrumental *and* value rational action. He calls this a 'counter-factual' standard for the obvious reason that it stands, against the factual reality of the present order, as the criterion for a yet-to-be-achieved and more rational future social order with a different organizational principle.

THE 'CRISES' OF LEGITIMATION, MOTIVATION AND THE STATE

In Chapter 2 we saw that societies either disintegrate or pass from one stage of evolution to another higher stage when their organizational framework ('the organizational principle') changes in the face of strains with which the whole social system can no longer cope. 'Crisis' is the now fashionable term that describes the condition of a society that is hard up against its own survival limits. Is late capitalist society at just this point? What are the limits to 'more of the same' and to further progress premised on a reliance on the same basic mode of social organization?

It is from this perspective that we should read Habermas's *Legitimation Crisis,* the best-known statement of his political sociology of advanced capitalist societies. This work is more clearly marxist than much of his other writing. Certainly Habermas still sees the relation between wage labour and capital as the basic organizational principle both of liberal capitalist *and,* albeit in a modified form, of late capitalist society as well. Despite important differences between the two, the organization of the society is still irrationally geared to capital accumulation and hence to the private interests of a few rather than, rationally, to general or collective interests and needs.

Yet orthodox marxist categories are no longer adequate to explain contemporary late capitalism. Of the several changed circumstances that need explanation, one of the most important is that exploitation is increasingly mediated through a state apparatus to the point now where disadvantage and misery are more often associated with such factors as sickness, age, race, regional geography and gender than with class position strictly assessed in terms of a labour theory of value—a notion that is undermined both by the eclipse of the factory model as the principal means of economic exploitation and also, among other things, by the enormous productive force of science, technology and 'information' that no longer allows any plausible measure of the profit that is extracted from each worker (how do you measure the labour power in such an abstract thing as a computer program?).

These considerations ask for a theory that both takes account of the enormously expanded role of the State in late capitalist society and comes to terms as well with the altered basis of power and domination in relatively affluent mass democracies where participation and assent are, apparently, no longer related to the blind compulsion of 'work or starve' that was typical in earlier periods of liberal capitalism. *Legitimation Crisis* may be read as an attempt to deal with these difficulties and as an attempt, also, to relate such other key notions as revolution and alienation to the changed circumstances of late capitalism. Revolution conceived in the classical way after the French and the Russian experience as the forcible seizure of power no longer makes sense in the context of late capitalist society. One may therefore ask whether Marx's explanatory intentions are better served, in our situation, with a theory of a crisis with 'transformative effects' that have the potential to change the organizational principle of society. For the same reason it will be useful to reconsider what the classical marxist concept of alienation could mean in our contemporary situation: is the explanatory intention of the concept obscured or resuscitated by a crisis theory that explains the failure of legitimation and of motivation as consequences of power relations that destroy the social fabric of interaction, solidarity, identity and communication?

The basic theorems
In *Legitimation Crisis* Habermas's political sociology is developed against the background of a general systems theory framework. Its relation to the rest of his work will be clearer if the book is read, firstly, as a preliminary attempt to specify, in a systematic way, the character and limits of the rationalization process in Weber's negative sense of the 'Iron Cage', secondly, as the nucleus of Habermas's important contributions to the theory of the modern (late capitalist) state and, thirdly, as I have suggested, the focus for some of his differences with orthodox marxism. With the next several pages I shall describe the basic outlines of that work, then focus on the problem of the State before considering challenges to Habermas's formulations.

In the first formulations the systems model has three sub-systems as set out in Fig. 6 below [13].

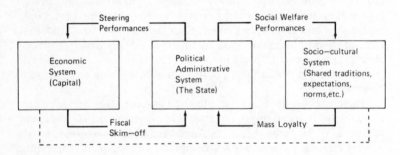

Fig. 6.

The economic sub-system, which we may construe more simply as the ensemble of privately owned capitalist enterprises, produces goods and services for profit. It is assumed further, that capital, in late capitalist societies, depends for its support and maintenance on a large state apparatus ('the political administrative sub-system') that must provide 'steering performances': the state must 'steer' the economy in such a way as to provide favourable conditions for economic growth. However, one of the defining characteristics of a capitalist state is that it is *excluded* from private production for profit—that is the basis for the common distinction between the private and public sectors. For this reason it is *dependent* for its revenues on taxes that are levied on the private economy—dependent on 'the fiscal skim off'. On the other side, the state must maintain popular assent and mass loyalty. In order to do this it must use its fiscal revenues to provide social, educational and welfare services and to support the ideology (the 'technocratic consciousness' and the like) that *legitimates* the whole system. This is a necessary (but not a sufficient) condition for the maintenance, 'in' the sociocultural sub-system, of all those norms, attitudes, values and 'action-motivating meanings' that secure conformity with political, legal, and social domination in the larger system of society as a whole. The thrust of Habermas's work will be to show that this is more problematic than its seems.

In *Legitimation Crisis* Habermas argues that a crisis may occur if any one of the sub-systems fails to produce 'the requisite quantity' [14] of what it contributes to the whole. Accordingly, there are four possible crisis tendencies that are represented as follows [15]:

Point of origin (sub-system)	System crisis	Identity crisis
Economic	Economic crisis	—
Politico-admin.	Rationality crisis	Legitimation crisis
Sociocultural	—	Motivation crisis

The system is such that an attempt to control crises in one sub-system results in the transformation and displacement of inherent contradictions into another. For example, an economic crisis could, hypothetically, be controlled with large handouts of state funds to shore up some key area of capital accumulation: the automobile industry or the banking sector, for example; but this may well both expose the partiality of the state towards vested capital intersts and at the same time force an offsetting reduction of welfare spending and so increase the legitimation deficit. As Ronge notes: 'The question might emerge which side—accumulation (economy) or legitimacy (demands of the social system)—is the driving force . . . (in the development of crisis) [16].

I do not propose to say much about the 'economic crisis' [17] because there is nothing particularly original or significant in this aspect of Habermas's scheme. His formulation of the rationality crisis owes much to the work he did with Claus Offe, among others, in the early 1970s and it is sufficient to note here that 'rationality crises' and 'rationality deficits' signal limits in the administrative production of rational decisions: they signal the failure of formal rationality (in the strictly Weberian sense) as a tool of social organization and they mark the fraying edges of a rationalization process that has run into limits beyond those that accrue simply from the overloading of the state's decision-making capacities [18].

It is Habermas's theorems of the legitimation and motivation crises that are original and centrally important. The two are, as Habermas concedes [19], thoroughly enmeshed inasmuch as a legitimation crisis would ensue from a failure of 'action-motivating meanings', i.e. from a motivation crisis. A fully blown legitmation crisis would threaten the whole of the state apparatus with disintegration and perhaps also produce either a change in the organizational principle of the society or else a regressive spate of authoritarian repression. In the face of rising levels of justification the threatening crisis is offset, buffered, or diffused with the expansion of the welfare state and the contrived legitimations of ritual parliamentary elections. In 1974 Habermas was still of the view that these compensatory processes were close to their limits. He claims broad agreement concerning the 'structural risks' that threaten first the state, and through it, the organization of the whole society [20].

> There is today no disagreement concerning the structural risks built into developed capitalist economies. These have to do primarily with interruptions of the accumulation process conditioned by the business cycle, the external costs of a private production that cannot adequately deal with the problem situations it itself creates, and a pattern of privilege whose core is a structurally conditioned unequal distribution of wealth and income. . ... The three great areas of responsibility against which the performance of the government is today measured are then: shaping a business policy that ensures growth, influencing the structure of production in a manner oriented to collective needs, and correcting the pattern of social inequality.

There are three main risks that can be listed and paired, as shown in Table 4, with corresponding 'responsibilities', or imperatives, which the State must obey in order to maintain the legitimacy of the existing social order.

Ideology was defined above to mean ideas that serve either to hide or to legitimate power, in other words, to hide, to normalize, in short to *legitimate* the underlying structure of social organization (the organizational principle)—which is still, as we have seen, the exploitation of one class to the advantage of another. Legitimation deficits accrue as this underlying irrationality is recognized—as rationality breaks in, so to speak—and as conformity and loyalty are shaken by the borad recognition that the system is geared to partial interests rather than to collective needs. A legitimation crisis threatens at the point where an ideologically secured and *pseudo*-legitimate [22] social consensus is revealed as naked power. It is also,

Table 4

'Structural risk' or crisis tendency	Basic 'responsibilities' of State, i.e. imperatives of state action necessary for the avoidance of crisis and the continuing legitimation of the existing structure
1. Interruptions to the capital accumulation process brought on at low points in the business cycle, i.e. 'economic crisis' that spills over into 'rationality crisis' and 'fiscal crisis of the state'[a]	State must shape business policy that ensures growth (e.g. with tax concessions, steered education, and labour policies, state-provided infrastructure — railways, telecommunications, publicly funded power stations for privately owned aluminium smelters, etc.)
2. Social costs and problems created by private investment and accumulation, e.g. unemployment arising from migration of capital and from spread of high technology	State must influence production in a way which either compensates the disadvantaged and/or serves collective needs, (e.g. through protection, wages policy, and subsidies, etc.)
3. Structurally conditioned inequality threatens democratic norms of equality and reward for achievement	State must correct the pattern of inequality and the unequal distribution of wealth (e.g. with welfare assistance for disadvantaged ethnic, regional, and other groups)

[a]See title of O'Connor's book [21].

among other things, the point at which the masking effect of the 'technocratic consciousness' fails.

The originality of Habermas's contribution to the burning debate about the State and its problems should now be clear enough. He attempts to specify the limits—to state action, political authority, and ultimately to capitalism itself—that are encountered at the 'seam' between the State and the sociocultural order. As we have seen, these limits are grounded in the evolution of society: and they should be seen as part of the close-up detail of a longer world-historical process of rationalization.

In these late capitalist societies legitimation is limited, broadly, in at least two different ways. Limits are set by the degraded but still latent and undissolved elements of the bourgeois public sphere. Civil law, legal norms of due process, the natural rights of the individual, the common assumptions of citizenship, and of freedom of assembly and speech, politcal and religious freedom and indeed the very notion of 'free exchange' in a 'free market' are all part of what we call 'formal democracy' [23]. Of course, all of these things are used covertly to manipulate public opinion and to hide the real structures of power with a pseudo-legitimacy. Habermas's argument developed and anchored, as we have seen in other contexts, is that these normative structures of 'formal democracy' contain precisely within their *forms,* a residue that is not without 'structure-forming effects'—or, perhaps more appropriately here, 'structure-*limiting* effects'. Public opinion is not now, and never could be, an entirely plastic substance that can be bent, shaped and coloured to meet any and every legitimation deficit. The gains of the eighteenth and nineteenth centuries still have an effective institutional embodiment within just these *'forms' of democracy* and they are manifest now in a raised 'level of justification' such that: 'Only the rules and communicative presuppositions that make it possible to distinguish an accord or agreement among free and equals from a contingent or forced consensus have legitimating force today' [24]. Moreover, we find this raised level of justification, and with it further limits to legitimation, present in what Habermas calls the *'communicative ethics'* of late capitalist society. He says that: 'Before norms of domination could be accepted without reasons by the bulk of the population, the communication structures in which our motives for action have till now been formed would have to be thoroughly destroyed' [25]. He is pointing here to the fact that we—you and I and most people in these advanced capitalist societies—normally resolve doubts, and disagreements about what ought to be done (in ordinary social relations and in the public sphere) with free argument and discussion—and not normally with magic, prayer, knives, or pistol shots. And again normally (it's the *norms* that matter) these mundane arguments and discussions have a particular *form* inasmuch as the participants reciprocally assume the right to question the grounds and motives of those who affirm contrary positions to their own. The discussion and the level of justification have become reflective. It is in this way that discussion, or more particularly, its raised level of justification has become reflective and of course this is how rational 'critique' finds its way into ordinary social interaction. Agreement and clarifications that are reached in this way produce genuine conviction and commitments that seem to hold firm over a noticeably broad range of specific contexts and situations. In other words they have 'a rationally motivating force' and 'structure-forming effects' that limit and define, potentially at least, what can and cannot claim legitimacy.

Different limits are set, and other legitimation and motivation deficits are piled up, through the dysfunctional side-effects of development in late capitalist societies. Here Habermas is on strong and familiar ground. Initially he simply recapitulates the commonplace fact that the accelerating effects of modernization and development have everywhere led to increasing urbanization, industrialization, and, in the case of the most 'advanced' and developed societies, to all those further developments that mark the so-called 'post-industrial' society. The more obvious effects of all these developments are universally accepted. Everyone agrees that economic development and the expansion of market relations has been accompanied everywhere by the disintegration of local community neighbourhoods, of extended family structures, and of the more settled forms of church and religion. Together with the residues of traditional worldviews, all these institutions *once used to* guarantee social reproduction and social integration. Habermas's argument is that now they are either spent or endangered sources of social integration and, accordingly, that motivation and legitimation deficits accrue in several ways.

Firstly, as the 'traditionalist padding' is stripped away, politically effective legitimations are not so easily conjured up from myths and motivating symbols such as; 'Land of Opportunity', 'The Flag', King, God, Country, *'Religion, Patrie, Famille'*, and the like. His argument is that as we move still further along the course of late capitalism the store of once-powerful collective self-representations are dried up by the technocratic consciousness and reduced to notions of a mechanistically conceived economic growth, and that they are then no longer effective in sustaining the legitimacy of the whole structure in the same unproblematic way.

Second, less dramatic and more significant legitimation deficits arise as broad areas of policy and administration that once depended for their taken-for-granted legitimacy on these now spent traditions are 'explicitly thematized' and so exposed to widening contestation. As we shall see in a moment, he will, in his later work, call this the 'colonization of the lifeworld'. The best example is education [26] to which Habermas refers in the following way [27]:

> The boundaries of the political system, *vis-à-vis* the cultural system shift . . . .. In this situation, cultural affairs that were once taken for granted, and were previously boundary conditions for the political system, fall into the administrative planning area. Thus traditions withheld from the public problematic, and all the more from practical discourses, are thematised. An example of such direct administrative processing of cultural tradition is educational planning, especially curriculum planning. Whereas school administrators formerly [only] had to codify a canon that had taken shape in an unplanned nature-like manner, present curriculum planning is based on the premise that traditional patterns could as well be otherwise. Administrative planning produces a universal pressure for legitimation [in an area which was] once distinguished precisely for its power of self-legitimation.

Third, as the older institutions and traditions fail, the state is expected to carry the burdens of social integration. This results in what Daniel Bell called 'the revolution of entitlements' and, in Habermas's view, an *irreducible* dependency upon the provisions of the welfare state [28]—for education, social security, health, transport, legal services, housing and the like as well as for 'law and order', state-supported childcare, and other measures to offset the diminishing capacities of families. The deficits accrue not only because the state is faced on the one side with these increasing demands and, on the other side, with the conflicting demands of capital for reduced taxes, deregulation, and cuts in welfare and public spending. The deficits accrue for the further reason that simple 'allocative policies' (of allocating specific resources to specific claimants) are, at best, only palliatives that do nothing to redress the underlying structural inequalities. More problematically still, they bring to the surface of political contestation a welter of contradictory demands that are then met with smoothing and avoidance strategies that are impossible to coordinate successfully beyond the short term and that ultimately only add to the frustrations, suspicions and resentments of large populations.

Fourth, as disturbed traditions are exhausted or torn out of their interpretative contexts, other more 'psychological' costs are accumulated. Rationalization of this negative kind produces what Durkheim first called 'anomie'. It is not only that spent traditions leave the individual without consolation in the face of natural contingencies (of sickness, accident, bereavement etc.) although that is certainly significant. Habermas's stronger claim is that the sanity, well-being, and the very identity of each individual ultimately depends on shared, or at least, reciprocally communicable, self-understandings, upon 'ego-defining structures', that join up your inner world with mine in such a way as to make mutual understanding, negotiation and relationship possible. Habermas insists that the desiccation of traditions, the manipulation of worldviews, forced social change, and the forced acceptance of carrot-'n-stick inducements all combine to distort 'the communicative structures' and 'ego-securing' structures upon which mass loyalty and generalized motivations of the population depend.

I have outlined some of the crisis tendencies that arise especially at the interface with the sociocultural order. It must not be inferred from this abbreviated outline of *some* of the limits and deficits that there is anything narrowly deterministic or mechanical in Habermas's formulation. On the contrary, he carefully explains that there is no way of predicting the type or form, and certainly not the outcome, of a crisis; and that the organizational structure of capitalist society is protected through the depoliticizing and neutralizing effects of scientism and of 'familial and vocational privatization'. Both are clearly very effective. The technocratic consciousness continues to dissolve the residues of the public sphere and to screen off the forced adaptation of family life, education, and other facets of the socialization process, to the demands of capital accumulation—for the intensification of work and the assignment of the social costs of production to wage and salary earners, to the unemployed and to women and minorities. And similarly, it is clear that these same economic demands of the the business sector are, for the time being, well able to dissolve the value-rational (*wertrational*) core of older vocational orientations [29] through a steady intensification of possessive individualism and of the achievement ideology.

Does this mean that these limts and the deficits are completely misconceived or that they are simply more elusive than we had first supposed?

Some problems and challenges

Among the many and varied challenges that Habermas has drawn from his critics [30] some are especially important because they point beyond technical and methodological problems to the more basic clash of paradigms that have come to the surface in the debates that he has entered. In the following comments I can do no more than allude to the paradigmatic outlines of some of these challenges and discussions.

(1) It is the challenge of Luhmann's [31] radical functionalism that has had the greatest long-term effect on Habermas's own formulations and revisions. Luhmann's charge is that the very assumption that modern (late capitalist) societies can be understood, organized or governed either by their citizens or in terms of a rational or normative consensus is nothing more than an old-fashioned and untenable illusion of 'old European' liberal democracy. Societies can no longer reproduce or govern themselves in this way because they are too complex. These societies cope with uncertainty in a completely different and nearly opposite way: they deal with uncertainty by the selection, and then the differentiation and isolation, of problems that would otherwise spread, 'like fire in a box of matches', from one cell of the system to others. Rationality no longer has anything to do with rational discourse or with practical decisions about what we should or should not do. Rationality is a property *not* of the individual or of interacting subjeects but of the *system*; more precisely it is the measure of that system's adaptation to its environment. In the words of Luhmann's subtle provocations, 'Three millennia of the individual have come to a close': 'As the accelerated growth of complexity makes it necessary for society to convert to a form of reproduction that gives up the differentiation between power and truth in favour of a nature-like development withdrawn from reflection' [32]. In this view of course, power dissolves truth and the public becomes the object rather than the subject of politics. This is Weber's Iron Cage made perfect and transposed into cybernetics and systems theory. Administration and planning must confine decision choices in whatever measure is necessary to

reduce complexity and increase the steering capacity (adaptability) of the society in the face of its environment. Habermas responds to these challenges, in *Legitimation Crisis,* and with respect, specifically, to late capitalist societies, with the argument that the total administration of society is impossible for the reason that [33]:

> the scope of action of the administrative system . . . [is]
> . . . limited on *two* sides: in steering the economic sector, by the parameters of a property order that it cannot change; in creating motivation, by independent (*eigensinnig*) development of normative structures that are irreconcilable with the suppression of generalisable interests.

His larger argument is that *social integration is independently rooted in the development of worldviews and of normative structures that do not reduce to the requirement of system integration.* What Luhmann does not see is that legitimations, commands, and ideas are all loaded with validity claims that we accept more or less unthinkingly. The point is that motivation, participation, and conforming loyalty *all* depend ultimately on our shared and taken-for-granted assumption that validity claims implicit in every administrative and social action *could,* in principle, be made good or, 'discursively redeemed' in a rational discourse that is ultimately beyond manipulation.

At the deepest level, motivation is tied to reason. Socialization is the 'adaptation of "inner nature" to Society' [34]. But it is an adaptation to a society that is not reducible to a technology of information management or to administrative and governmental structures, because society is *also* a lifeworld of—choose your own preferred labels: 'normative structures' or 'ego-defining interpretative systems' (our translations of Habermas's terms); or 'symbolic interaction' (Mead); or a 'controlling symbolic' (Rieff); or 'meaningful forms', or simply 'culture' (Geertz). The lifeworld that gives form and content to ego-identity *develops according to its own logic,* and it is for just this reason that our lives and actions do not reduce to a simple product of the system: as Habermas insists, social integration is *not* 'at the disposition of the imperatives of power augmentation' [35].

(2) Whereas Habermas insists that the legitimacy of the political order depends on a 'normatively secured social identity' it is certainly possible to object that this is a vastly overloaded notion and that participation and acceptance are instead motivated only by the more ordinary pragmatic and utilitarian motives of individuals who are typically content to 'play the system' for their own ends. These objections are familiar: they are grounded in other political philosophies—in moral scepticism, classical liberalism, and British utilitarianism—that are opposed to the first premises

of Habermas's Kantian and Hegelian tradition. They lead among other things to the objection that the individual's relationship to the political order is no different from his or her relationship with the organization in which he or she may work as an employee. In both cases the relationship is essentially contractual and secured on the one side by inducements [36] and on the other by calculations of individual benefit and advantage.

From Habermas's point of view, the flaw in the several variants of these arguments is that they all tend to minimize or to deny that the terms of exchange, the contract itself, and the criteria that the individual uses to reckon the benefits are *all* set within a political culture and 'normative structures' that have causal effects — effects that are more or less fragile, more or less susceptible to disturbance. The blind assumption that political action and personality are *not* pre-defined by political culture and normative structures is simply a reassertion of the untenable liberal dogma that all social forms are epi-phenomenal to the individual. On the other hand, insofar as these objections do accept that the actions, choices, and cognitive orientations of the individual are at least partly coordinated through group norms and cultural referents then the arguments move straight away back into Habermas's court and must again face his challenge, namely, that these critics should specify how, and in what respects, social forms set limits on the economy and the State.

(3) Another objection is that 'deskilling' [37], new work practices, and new forms of 'scientific management' have already atomized the workforce in a way that invisibly secures control from above. I think the argument here is that power is so effectively embodied in the material design and application of technology, control, and production as to give the lie to alternative theorizations of domination by normative structures. These arguments do usefully direct attention to the newer forms of exploitation that typify advanced capitalist societies. However, it is important to recognize them for what they are, namely new and sometimes convincing attempts to rescue what Habermas calls the 'paradigm of production' of orthodox marxism (together with the labour theory of value) and, within these discussions of 'work practices' and the like, to reduce problems of power, social structure and social integration, to a strictly economic calculation of the relation between capital and labour. At another level the effect is to ignore, or implicitly to deny, Habermas's central assertion that these new work practices must, at some point, run up against limits that are independently rooted in normative structures and affirmed in the necessity to maintain social integration.

(4) A further objection is that Habermas's emphasis upon the socially integrative function of normative structures, upon 'generalizable interests' as opposed to partial interests, and upon solidarity and consensus, var-

iously understates, obscures, or denies the plurality of groups and interests that is so characteristic of late capitalist society. In these objections there is more than an occasional doubt that Habermas is in some way trying to normatively resuscitate other 'old European' social forms; of '*Gemeinschaft*' or, in Durkheim's terms, 'mechanical solidarity'. Habermas's response to these doubts [38] is that he has no problem at all with the plurality of interests and with a certain natural heterogeneity of conflicting interests among groups — the aged, ethnic minorities, homosexuals, children, regional populations—all with legitimate and particular interests of their own. His argument is that a critical social theory must use the *ideal* of 'generalizable interests' *critically*; that is to say as the 'counter-factual' criterion with which to confront psuedo-legitimate appeals to the common interest (as with appeals for sacrifices of real living standards 'in the interests of national economic development' etc.). His theory has no prescriptive programmatic content and points strictly to the *forms* of communication that offer the best chances for achieving collective and individual autonomy. The *content* and the structures that the participants create are for them to determine in their own situation. Nowhere does he concede an inch to the neo-conservative view [39] that consensus can or should be imposed, or that the plurality of empirical interests is somehow irrational or unworkable. Compromises are a politically acceptable and rational form of agreement in those cases where natural interests are incommensurate and thus preclude the possibility of creating new social solidarities with rational discourse.

(5) Challenges to Habermas from the French post-structuralist perspectives of Foucault and others also have a paradigmatic predictability. From these perspectives, the central criticism is that social action, 'communicative action' and 'communicative rationality', conceived in Habermas's way, are all faces of the same objectively given forms of power. Critical reflection is completely impotent; indeed the very possibility of critical reflection is an illusion because all forms of subjectivity, and of intersubjectivity, are, broadly speaking, merely the inner face of our subjection to power.

Habermas has always been careful to argue that the rational potential of the public sphere, of ideal speech, of rational discourse and now, most recently, of communicative reason is actualized only insofar as the interacting participants face one another in a situation that is *free of force*. The impact of these new attacks is, of course, the assertion that interaction is *never* free of structural force (power), and that 'rational discourse' is merely another means of securing it. At one level these objections do tell against Habermas because they force him to concede that the process of emancipation involves a kind of forcible 'break-in' to established circles of power. For Habermas this is theoretically problematic. Since rational discourse is not likely to arise from violence, how then do those who stand for a 'generalizable' interest break open the circle of those who oppress them? Certainly we need little proof of the obvious fact that class-bound inequalities do not readily yield to confrontation with rational argument.

Habermas's defence is firstly to concede the same ground as he has conceded, in a different context, to Luhmann, and namely to agree that power is indeed coordinated 'behind our backs' and that it comes in upon us 'from the outside in' as an impersonal structuring force that is both empirically effective and, for the most part, beyond conscious reckoning. However, what he does *not* concede is the epistemological and ontological definitions of power as comething that is, *a priori,* beyond conscious reason. Habermas is bound to reject these misconceived philosophical notions of power as a thing-in-itself as positivist illusions that are now represented anew in metatheoretical disguises.

LIFEWORLD AND SYSTEM

In the *Theory of Communicative Action* Habermas has transposed the theory of society into the paradigm of communication. This work is conceived as a second attempt to incorporate Max Weber into the spirit of Western marxism. Much is incorporated also from reconstructions of Durkheinm, Mead, and Parsons. Most importantly in this context the work resolves the objections that Habermas has had not only to Luhmann (a former student of Parsons) but also to many of systems theory's concepts of social reproduction, power, and coordination—all of which seem outwardly opposed to Habermas's Enlightenment project of emancipation and (positive) rationalization.

In his search for more comprehensive constructions of society Habermas has constantly attacked reductive and 'one-sided' explanations that reduce social phenomena to the 'base', to social structural and systems imperatives alone, and to the 'externalist perspective' that denies social action. Rather than simply rejecting these explanation he has tried always to remedy their one-sidedness by counterposing explanations that are set instead within the 'internalist perspective' of hermeneutically reconstructible understanding; within the developmental inner logic of worldviews and, subsequently from the perspective of social integration (as opposed to systems integration). In the preceding section we saw that legitimation and motivation deficits accumulate as phenomena from the one side are met with inflexible limits that are set in the other.

In the *Theory of Communicative Action* [40] Habermas joins these two perspectives—internalist and externalist—in a different way under the concepts of lifeworld and system respectively.

On the one hand, he constructs a communicatively shared *lifeworld*. The lifeworld is defined to contain the background of shared meaning that makes ordinary symbolic interaction possible and, further, it now explicitly includes also those structural components (institutions, normative structures, and social practices) that make social reproduction possible. These features are outlined in Table 5. The general features of this side of the

Table 5 — Contributions of reproduction processes to maintaining the structural components of the lifeworld [41]

Reproduction processes	Structural components		
Cultural reproduction	Interpretative schemata susceptible to consensus ('valid knowledge')	Legitimations	Behavioural pat terns influential in self-formation, educational goals
Social integration	Obligations	Legitimately ordered interpersonal relations	Social memberships
Socialization	Interpretative accomplishments	Motivation for norm-conformative actions	Capability for inter- action ('personal identity')

picture are easy enough to grasp. In the first place (row one of Table 5) it is clear that we are born into a symbolic world of meanings and that we repair, elaborate, change and integrate the contents of this symbolic world through the ordinary process of communicative action—through processes of agreement, discussion, and negotiation that go on all the time in ordinary social interaction. With their communicative actions, interacting individuals also share a stock of knowledge that provides the background for the legitimation of society as well as for self-formation. In a parallel way (row two), social integration reproduces obligations, legitimately ordered interpersonal relations and psychological representations of social memberships and affiliations. And, (row three) through the process of socialization with competent reference persons, children internalize a lifeworld that allows them to interpret meanings in a reliable fashion and they learn to conform with social norms and to interact with others in a way that reciprocally secures identity [42].

On the other hand, with his revised and developed concept of *system* [43] Habermas makes enormous concessions to Luhmann and to the systems theory 'paradigm'. It is with this concept of system that he comes to terms with the complexity and the elaborately differentiated structures of roles that are so characteristic of late capitalist society. Roughly speaking the system refers to those vast tracts of modern society that are 'uncoupled' from communicatively shared experience in ordinary language and *coordinated, instead, through the media of money and power*. Money is of course the archetypal steering medium. With his reconstructions of Marx, Habermas seeks to show how large areas of the lifeworld—the public sphere, education, citizenship and the like—have been 'mediatized': and that is to say dissolved and then reconstituted as imperatives of the economic subsystem. Power is a less perfect medium because it is inflexibly tied to bureaucratic roles and hierarchies that are less 'nature-like' and more easily comprehended in communicatively shared understanding. But, despite these differences, power still functions as a steering medium that takes over areas of the lifeworld and then reconstitutes them as the objects of state control. In terms of our earlier discussion it is these two media that shape and extend the 'technocratic consciousness'. The connections with Marx and Weber are easy to see. Money converts concrete labour into an abstract commodity in a 'free' market economy (the process of commodification) while power converts value-rational (*wertrational*) and practical action into the 'nature-like' imperatives of Weber's Iron Cage (the process of 'negative' rationalization conceived in the usual Weberian way). Both media coordinate and 'behaviorize' action by 'steering it' with imperatives that have all the characteristics of what Durkheim called 'social facts'—they coordinate action 'from the outside in', with obligatory force, and in a 'nature-like' way that is inaccessible to reflection through lived experience recalled and shared in ordinary social interaction.

Basically Habermas invites us to look at our own modern condition as a kind of tug-of-war between the lifeworld and the system. Communicative rationality can only arise in the lifeworld as an achievement of communicative reason that might, eventually, lead to more rational structures (to authority without fear or exploitation and thus to changed organizational principles that would be based on the interests of all and so deserve the genuine legitimacy of consensual agreements). Every painful step in this direction involves a linguistification of reified (nature-like) system structures that have to be re-appropriated through communicative action into the lifeworld. Given the unyielding organizational principle of capitalist society, the lifeworld is, from the other direction, constantly subjugated to mediatized colonization by the economy and the state (money and market, power and bureaucracy, respectively).

The crisis tendencies and deficits that were first analysed in *Legitimation Crisis* reappear now (in a changed and more developed explanatory framework) *at the 'seam' between the system and the lifeworld.* Through the steering media of money and power, social relations in the lifeworld are monetarized and bureaucratized—'juridification' (*Verrechtlichung*) is Habermas's word for the latter process—and thus relentlessly adapted to the functional requirements of the system. However, this *colonization of the lifeworld* strikes back at the whole process of rationalization and becomes pathological when it endangers the symbolic reproduction of society. This is, for example, precisely what happens as consumerism and competitive individualism create such intense pressures for 'achievement' and for the utilitarianization of all values that family structures collapse under the pressure and/or produce other pathological side-effects in gender relations and the like. In a similar way, the 'juridification' of client and citizen roles through the welfare state turns acting subjects and rightful claimants into dependent objects of bureaucratic regulation in a way that impairs autonomy, psychological health, and symbolically structured affiliations and memberships. The pathological effects of colonization may so undermine communicative action in other such specific and functionally vital areas as higher administration and policy formation [44] as to make coherent and consistent performance very problematic indeed. For the moment it is enough simply to allude to the several disturbances in the reproduction of society that are caused by the pathological effects of this colonization of the lifeworld (Table 6).

Table 6 — Crisis phenomena connected with disturbances in reproduction [45]

Disturbances in the domain of	Structural components (of the lifeworld)		
	Culture	Society	Person
Cultural reproduction	Loss of meaning	Withdrawal of legitimation	Crisis in orientation and education
Social integration	Insecurity of collective identity	Anomie	Alienation
Socialization	Breakdown of tradition	Withdrawal of motivation	Psychopathologies

The great achievement of Habermas's political sociology is that it offers a multi-dimensional view of politics. The more obvious political conflicts that find expression through parliamentary and other formal structures of politics (trade unions, politcal parties, formal associations and interest groups etc.) and that centre on problems of distribution, national security, economic development, law and order and the like are now, in Habermas's political sociology, examined in a perspective that *systematically incorporates the causal effects of changes and disturbances in the sociocultural order with those that arise in the economy and the State.* With this larger framework Habermas is able to address the new and completely different forms of political conflict that arise, at 'the seam between the system and the lifeworld' [46].

> In the last ten to twenty years, conflicts have developed in advanced western societies that, in many respects, deviate from the welfare-state pattern of institutionalized conflict over distribution. These new conflicts no longer arise in areas of material reproduction; they are no longer channelled through parties and organizations; and they can no longer be alleviated by compensations that conform to the system. Rather, the new conflicts arise in areas of cultural reproduction, social integration, and socialization. They are manifested in sub-institutional, extra-parliamentary forms of protest. The underlying deficits reflect a reification of communicative spheres of action; the media of money and power are not sufficient to circumvent this reification. The question is not one of compensations that the welfare state can provide. Rather, the question is now to defend or reinstate endangered life styles, or how to put reformed life styles into practice. In short, the new conflicts are not sparked by *problems of distribution,* but concern *the grammar of forms of life.*

Liberal, pluralist, corporatist and orthodox marxist theories of politics are quite unable to satisfactorily explain or evaluate these new conflicts, claims, and resistances that now typically find expression in the environmental movement, the peace movement, and the women's movement, as well as in new forms of religious fundamentalism, worker cooperatives, and communes, and in a range of new psychotherapies and alternative lifestyles.

In the light of Habermas's theory this otherwise confusing array of phenomena takes on a new significance as differing political responses of the one-sidedness of the rationalization process. In the case of fundamentalist religious movements, the colonization of the lifeworld typically produces a convulsive closure against all the possibilities of modernity. On the other hand, and in the case of the most progressive elements of the feminist movement, we see that, as the same process of colonization has undermined the social reproduction of gender, a potential for reason has been 'released' and taken up with claims for equality that are explicitly based on universalistic principles and aimed at the particularism and the exploitative practices of established power interests.

The outcome of this 'dialectic' between system and lifeworld cannot be predicted. It may be that the problems which break out at the seam between the lifeworld and the system will be resolved in favour of the system through improved steering performances that reduce the 'burdens' of consciousness, deliberation, and decision. On the other hand, the utopian hopes that surface from a lifeworld stripped of its traditional strictures may, through new forms of communicative action, regenerate a degraded public sphere and produce new 'communicatively achieved agreements' with new 'structure-forming effects'.

NOTES

[1] CES, p. 199.
[2] See 'Limitation Problems in the Modern State', in CES.
[3] The translation is to appear in 1987 in the series edited by Tom McCarthy and published by MIT Press.
[4] From Montesquieu, Rousseau and de Tocqueville among others.
[5] I am indebted to Jean Cohen and Andrew Arato's excellent paper 'Civil Society and Social Theory' presented in February 1986 at a conference in London. The papers are to appear in a book on Civil Society edited by John Keane.
[6] J. Habermas, 'The Public Sphere: An Encyclopedia Article (1964)', originally appearing in Fischer Lexicon *Staat und Politik,* new edition, Frankfurt am Main, 1964, pp. 220–226, and subsequently in *New German Critique,* **1**, 3, 1974, pp.49–55.
[7] See Peter Hohendahl's exposition and evaluation of the German reception of this early work in his, 'Critical Theory, Public Sphere and Culture: Jürgen Habermas and his Critics', *New German Critique,* **16**, Winter, 1979, pp. 89–118.
[8] For a very readable overview that is especially important as a background to Habermas's political sociology see Part 4 of Max Weber's *General Economic History.*
[9] Gianfranco Poggi, *The Development of the Modern State: A Sociological Introduction,* Stanford University Press, 1978, Ch. 6 and p. 107. This book provides a general and accessible discussion of the context of Habermas's political sociology. See also a forthcoming work on the State that Poggi is to publish in the 'Key Ideas' series.
[10] For a review of the criticisms see Hohendahl (note [7]).
[11] Bottomore has, among others, made these criticisms in T. Bottomore,

The Frankfurt School (Key Sociologists series), Ellis Horwood, Chichester, 1984, and Habermas has accepted them in Jürgen Habermas, 'A Philosophico-Political Profile', *New Left Review,* **151**, 1985, pp. 75–105.

[12] Jürgen Habermas, *Towards a Rational Society* (hereafter TRS), trans. J. J. Shapiro, Heinemann, London, 1971, pp. 112–113.

[13] My adaptation of an early working model that Habermas takes from Claus Offe, 'Krise und Krisemanagement' in Janicke, *Herrschaft und Krise*, p. 197ff. See LC, p. 5. In the explanations that I offer below I use, for the sake of simplicity, the terms 'dependence', 'exclusion', and 'maintenance' in a way that accords more closely with Claus Offe. See especially C. Offe, 'The Theory of the Capitalist State and the Problem of Policy Formation', and also, 'Introduction to Legitimacy Versus Efficiency', both in Lindberg, Alford, Crouch and Offe (eds) *Stress and Contradiction in Modern Capitalism,* Heath and Co., New York, 1975.

[14] LC, p. 49.

[15] LC, p. 45.

[16] Volker Ronge, 'The Politicization of Administration in Advanced Capitalist Societies', *Political Studies,* **22**, March 1974.

[17] See J. O'Connor, *The Fiscal Crisis of the State,* St. Martin's Press, New York, 1973.

[18] This theory of the 'overloading' of the state with too many decisions is presented, in its conservative liberal version, in *Crisis of Democracy: Report on the Governability of Democracies to the Trilateral Commission,* New York University Press, 1975. See especially Part One. Habermas endorses the criticisms of these views offered by J. Heidorn, *Legitimität und Regierbarkeit,* 1982, p. 249.

[19] In Habermas's reply to his critics in, *Habermas: Critical Debates,* John B. Thompson and David Held, (eds), Macmillan, London, 1982, pp. 280–281.

[20] CES, p. 194.

[21] O'Connor, *The Fiscal Crisis of the State,* (see note [17]).

[22] Habermas explains, unambiguously, that genuine legitimacy means 'a political order's worthiness to be recognised', CES, p. 178.

[23] In contradistinction presumably to 'substantive' or, in Habermas's terms, rational democracy in which there would be authority without fear and no deception.

[24] CES, p. 188.

[25] CES, p. 188.

[26] M. Pusey, 'The Legitimation of State Education Systems', *Australian & N.Z.J. of Sociology,* **16**/2, 1980; and 'Rationality Organisation and

Language', *Thesis Eleven,* No. 10/11, Nov.–Mar. 1984–85, pp. 89–110.

[27] LC, p. 71.

[28] It is here that Habermas's argument seems somewhat too closely based on the experience of an affluent West Germany. And of course this was all written before Fraser, Thatcher and Reagan demonstrated how savagely these provisions can be attacked with apparent impunity in the short term.

[29] The residue of the Protestant Ethic in 'the methodical conduct of life' and to other related value-rational elements in the orientation of what Weber calls 'the man of vocation'. See preceding discussion in Chapter 2.

[30] For an excellent sample see, *Habermas: Critical Debates,* John B. Thompson and David Held (eds), Macmillan, London, 1982.

[31] The debate is carried on at length in a book that Habermas and Luhmann wrote together for just this purpose under the title of *Theorie der Gesellschaft oder Sozialtechnologie,* Suhrkamp, Frankfurt, 1971. See also Niklas Luhmann, *The Differentiation of Society,* trans. S. Holmes and Charles Larmore, Colombia University Press, New York, 1982.

[32] LC, p. 136.

[33] LC, p. 135.

[34] LC, p. 13.

[35] LC, p. 8.

[36] Chester Barnard, *The Functions of the Executive,* Harvard University Press, Cambridge, MA, 1938.

[37] The term originates in a stream of literature that has followed H. Braverman's *Labor and Monopoly Capital: the Degradation of Work in the Twentieth Century,* Monthly Review Press, New York, 1974.

[38] Jürgen Habermas, 'A Philosophico-Political Profile', *New Left Review,* **151**, 1985, pp. 75–105.

[39] 'Neo-Conservative Culture Criticism in the United States and West Germany: An Intellectual Movement in Two Political Cultures', Jürgen Habermas, *Telos,* **56**, 1983. See also Habermas's several criticisms of the views of Arnold Gehlen in both LC and RRS.

[40] Thomas McCarthy's translation of the second volume, *Zur Kritik der funktionalistischen Vernunft* is scheduled to appear in 1987. In the meantime McCarthy's excellent synopsis of this second volume (to which I am indebted for many of the points in this discussion) is available in the latter part of his introduction to the first volume (i.e. RRS).

[41] Habermas in, Thompson and Held (eds), *Habermas: Critical Debates,* Macmillan, London, 1982, p. 279.

[42] *Theory of Communicative Action* (hereafter TCA) Vol. 2, p. 208 (see note [2] to Preface).

[43] Habermas reworks his concepts through a critical reconstruction of Parsons in the second volume of TCA.

[44] See my forthcoming study of The State (the title is still undetermined) that is to be published by Cambridge University Press in 1988.

[45] Adapted from Habermas, in Thompson and Held, p. 280 (see note [41]).

[46] *Theorie des kommunikativen Handelns,* Band 2, p. 576. This translation is taken from Jürgen Habermas, 'New Social Movements', *Telos,* **49**, 1981, pp. 33–37. A slightly different translation appears on p. xxxv in Tom McCarthy's excellent introduction to the whole work that is to be found in RRS.

Concluding comments

Habermas offers a 'Third Way' that synthesizes the creative residues of both liberal and marxist theories of society into a new and critical social theory. In many ways he stands 'betwixt and between' and must therefore run the gauntlet between these two positions and thus often attract that special kind of scorn that is reserved for those who first deeply understand, and then reject, our most deeply held convictions. There is nothing surprising in the growing and sometimes intense controversy that Habermas has provoked. Many of the critics in these and other competing perspectives have pressed Habermas to make useful and sometimes important changes and refinements.

I have alluded in the foregoing chapters to some of the criticisms that have come from empiricists, orthodox marxists, and post-structuralists and thus from the clashes with the other paradigms that Habermas has challenged. Now, with the following remarks, I would like to conclude with some appraisals that will help focus attention on the work a a whole.

AN EMPTY INTELLECTUALISM?

Every social theory contains its own utopia, its own images of the 'the good life', that all(?) might share inasmuch as the theory can define, motivate, guide, and realize its own 'practical promise'. Orthodox marxists' theories of society are premised on a classless community free of exploitation, and the contents of these images will define what action and practice shall mean within the compass of that theory and its many variants. Similarly, just about every religious and humanist theory of the human condition also carries its own 'specifications' for its realization 'in practice'. The same is true of counter-cultures, of the scientific community, and of old and new social movements.

A criticism often made of Habermas is that his attempt to rescue the rationalist heritage and to lead practice with reason has drowned in a self-regarding intellectualism that does not at all relate to the circumstances of ordinary people in advanced capitalism societies. I think there are two aspects to these criticisms.

In the first place, a question is raised as to whether this theory that lays such emphasis on argument and reflection can have its roots in anything more than the pleasure which some people take in contriving arguments about anything and everything. Perhaps it is really a theory about theories that is grounded only in some variant of the experience of doing research in an academy. In what kind of prospect is it grounded? What joy does it offer? [1].

What libidinous images does a theory have which is so abstract and which stands under an unbelievable compulsion to synthesise? Where in the intellectual work linked to it are moments of happiness, of satisfaction, without which one can hardly understand such effort?

The question invites a partly personal answer that Habermas gives informally, but in a most eloquent and illuminating way that is worth quoting at some length [2].

I have a conceptual motive and a fundamental intuition.... The motive-forming thought is the reconciliation of the decayed parts of modernity, the idea that without surrendering the differentiation that modernity has made possible in the social and economic spheres, one can find forms for living together in which real autonomy and dependency can appear in a satisfactory relation, that one can move erect in a collectivity that does not have the dubious quality of backward-oriented forms of community.... The intuition springs from ... experiences of undisturbed intersubjectivity. These are more fragile than anything that the history of communication structures has until now set into motion — a web of intersubjective relations that nevertheless make possible a relation between freedom and dependency that one can always only imagine with interactive models .... These ... ideas are always of successful interaction, of reciprocity and distance, of separation and manageable yet not failed nearness, of vulnerability and complementary caution. All of these images of protection, openness, and compassion, of submission and resistance rise out of a 'horizon of experience', to use Brecht's words, of 'friendly life together'. This friendliness does not exclude conflicts, rather it focusses on those human forms by way of which one can survive them.

This is Habermas's way of agreeing that, of course, the frozen stereo-types of 'academic' inquiry contain only misleading disembodied images of the place of reason in human affairs. Reasons, including those that are taken up by 'intellectuals', draw their 'libidinous' energy from the promise of community and from the successful communicative actions that they render possible.

The more stubborn critics who are not enticed or convinced by this approach to the theory/practice problem often press the criticism of intellectualism from another angle with the insistence that ordinary people do not have a taste for this sort of critically self-conscious interaction. Habermas's answer is that it is *not* a matter of choice. The circumstances of life in the modernity of late capitalism — of life amidst desiccated cultures, traditions and normative structures and an unrelenting pluralization and relativization of value orientations — force individuals to rely increasingly on their own 'communicative accomplishments'. As the security of relatively unproblematic agreement against an established background consensus recedes are 'ordinary people', Habermas insists, pressed further into an open-ended and critically reflective form of communicative interaction. A world-historical process of rationalization has, according to the theory, also released a potential for reason that *could be* actualized in new social structures mediated through communicative ethics. This possibility leads to other criticisms of the political sociology.

THE 'MOVEMENT OF REFLECTION' ... FORWARDS, UPWARDS AND SIDEWAYS, DOWNWARDS OR NOWHERE?

As we have seen, Habermas has gone to a great deal of effort to ground his view of modernity in a world-historical process of rationalization. The purpose was always to persuade us to re-assess our modern situation as a *one-sided development* and to help us recognize in its 'jagged profile' the traces of the other stunted lines of development that have been repressed. In a world-historical process of rationalization we have been brought to a situation in which we experience and then gradually discern the fundamental contradictions that are at work between, on the one hand, a truly positive (emancipatory) rationalization of ideas and ethics that points, in one direction, towards society, and, on the other hand, an increasing penetration of money and power that points instead to the 'Iron Cage' of a totally administered socity. This world-historical process of rationalization has, as Habermas puts it, 'released a potential for Reason' that could be taken up and used, in a critically reflective attitude, to build a more rational society. Or, alternatively, we could continue in the present course and destroy ourselves in any number of ways.

Certainly there is nothing naively deterministic in the theory. From the very beginnings of his enormous project Habermas has used all his brilliance in an attempt to reconcile the fundamental autonomy of thought and action with an evolutionary movement of reason in history that still has a clear Hegelian inspiration. His whole theory is an elaborate argument for his view that this process of reflection 'moves' simultaneously both, so to speak, 'forwards' and 'sideways'. On the one hand, as more settled traditional worldviews are fragmented and 'liquefied', we — you and I and everyone else — are together forced, to reach 'forwards' (and 'upwards'!) for understandings and agreements at *an ever higher level of abstraction and generality*. That is one way in which transcending reasons are institutionalized into our everyday lives — such an unBritish idea! At the same time, Habermas wants to argue that processes of reflection in any one of his three modes of action (cognitive, practical/normative, and expressive) help us to see 'over the fences' and beyond the 'one-sidedness' of our present orientation to life. In short, critical reflection achieved in one domain is supposed to release the 'repressed traces of reason' that are latent in the others [3] — put more crudely this is Habermas's way of arguing that 'depth' and 'breadth' are two faces of the one coin and that one leads to the other.

The reader who accepts these formulations at the general philosophical level may still have some difficulty in reconciling them with the political and social 'realities' of daily life in Reagan's America, Thatcher's Britain or Kohl's Germany. Habermas has always said that regression into a still deeper irrationality is always possible and this should be perfectly acceptable. So also should we accept his argument that competitive individualism, the 'achievement ethic' (an exquisite contradiction!), and the manipulated depolitization of the public sphere can indeed 'successfully' produce extra steering capacity for the system at the expense of all those who are caught in it. Yet these contemporary developments seem to offer some encouragement to the arguments of his empiricist conservative and liberal critics who argue that 'privatization', in both senses of the term, is the proper order of things and that motivation always boils down, at the individual level, to personal calculations of costs and benefits, and that, at the social level, these private calculations can reappear only in the 'reasons' that are at work in polling booths and the 'rationality' of markets — a very British idea.

Habermas's political sociology, and with it his whole theory, depend on his central argument that this pushing of problems back and forth between state and market must sooner or later run into limits set by the need for social reproduction and social integration. In short, he wants us to agree that the pain and the *confusions* that accrue from the side-effects of 'development' will both clear the way and at the same time lead the movement of reflection in a rational direction. It is the somewhat precarious grounding of this expectation in social-psychological arguments that encourages several conservative criticisms. Conservatives will argue, *firstly*, that the confusion and pain of a modernity stripped of all its 'traditionalistic padding' is more likely to have the opposite effect, and to produce instead an ever more blind inner dependence upon the authority of just those technocrats, cult leaders and charlatans who promise the simplest solutions (in Australia we are told that Reagan and his Marines make most Americans 'feel good' about themselves!). There is a further criticism, *secondly*, that the movement of reflection (in communicative action) to higher levels of generality and abstraction leads instead to an even greater instability of reference that will, as so often happens in the experimental situation of encounter groups, cause the participants either to drown in the new uncertainties they produce of else to fight over their bitter harvest of incommensurate splinters of meaning. And, *thirdly*, one can argue that the verbal and intellectual capacities needed to secure the necessary communicative accomplishments are so unevenly ditributed in any population that new forms of stratification will be created by the very effort to achieve equality.

Habermas understands these objectives perfectly well. He has always said that the future is inherently open and that there can be no theoretical guarantee of rational progress. He also makes the very reasonable answer that he has grounded his theory in the long historical time perspective of a world-historical process precisely so that it can hold fast against criticisms that are too easily influenced by arbitrary reactions to contemporary short-term trends. It is against this background that he has qualified many of the thrusts of *Legitimation Crisis* and accepted that the limits are more elastic than he had first assumed. And yet, every evolutionary theory does proffer its own kinds of predictions. Accordingly, we may need some rather more convincing transposition of ideas that may be more philosophically convincing than they are plausible in the sociopolitical domain into which they are aimed. We can agree with Habermas that, 'the shattering of naive consensus is the impetus for what Hegel calls, "the experience of reflection"' [4]. At the same time we can still ask him, not for a theoretical guarantee, but rather for greater reason to trust that the movement of reflection is, on the balance of probabilites, *more likely* to lead to communicatively achieved cooperation of a rational kind, and, conversely, that communicative reason has some immunity from dissolution into completely privatized mood states or into a more sinister dependence on the very kind of charismatic leaders that Habermas and his fellow Germans most fear. His 'critique of functionalist reason' [5] notwithstanding, Habermas must still show that communicative rationality has a better than even chance of success as a mode of social organization. Otherwise the way is open for empiricists and sceptics to revamp the old 'argument' that we are better off trusting what we have now.

AN INSUFFICIENTLY CRITICAL THEORY?

There is no space here to re-enter Habermas's reconstruction of Marx or to address the criticisms he has drawn from orthodox marxists. I want to consider only two points that recur among the more sympathetic of Habermas's critics who nonetheless doubt whether he is as critical of late capitalism as he should be.

(1) With *Knowledge and Human Interests*, Habermas attracted the sympathetic attention of many marxists because the work was addressed above all to the relationship between ideas and interests and therefore seemed, at least at first sight, to offer a new way of *unmasking interests*. *Legitimation Crisis* seemed to promise that this intention would be carried into the sphere of political sociology and eventually to practical matters.

It is entirely understandable that Habermas should have disappointed the many readers who in the 1980s might have been looking for a new theory language with which to uncover and 'read' the various ways in which capital is 'inscribed' in, organizational relations, in the family, 'the ideological state apparatus' and in other forms of late capitalism.

The point is that Habermas's initial intention in undertaking the project in the first place was to break just these positivistic connections between knowledge and interest that served as unquestioned first principles for many of his readers. From the very beginning Habermas set out to re-ground contemporary marxism first in a philosophical antropology and now in a general sociological theory that prohibits every easy economic reduction of ideas to interests (of capital). His intention was always to develop a vocabulary that would set the identification of particular, partial, arbitrary interests within a theory of *generalizable* or universal interests or, as he now puts it, of 'needs that can be communicatively shared'. For Habermas, the success of his own project depended on the ever-clearer specification of these universal interests and needs that are inherent in our social nature. In his view *that* is the surest way of exposing and 'unmasking' the selectivity, 'the one-sidedness', and the partiality of late capitalism's structures of power — and therefore also of guiding practice.

(2) Those who criticize Habermas for not adopting more militant positions are constantly perturbed by his own unwillingness to offer programs of reform and models for new institutional and organizational structures. The complaint is that he talks endlessly about theories, ideas,

and procedures and never about the structures that crush 'communicative rationality' and its would-be interlocutors before they can even choose their words.

In the main, Habermas's responses to these criticisms are clear and, I think, correct. His answer is that we must believe in democracy. Every attempt to write programs or social structures into the future pre-empts the communicative interaction that is the only source for the rationally motivated agreements that would make it liveable. The same answer holds right across the spectrum from the most muscular Leninist social engineering to the most gentle organizational designs for worker cooperatives and communes. New social and organizational structures, and indeed the very work of emancipation, grow out of communicative interaction. They are *cooperative achievements*. Indeed, Habermas gives the whole second volume of his new work to the 'critique of functionalist reason' so that he can muster still more comprehensive justifications for the positions he has taken against the functionalist reason of systems theory (of Parsons, Luhmann, and of the various new authority structures and tranquillizing myths with which neo-conservatives propose to secure the docility and submission of 'the masses'). He opposes every reduction of action to structurally coordinated controls that propose to shape our lives 'from the outside in' according to whatever formula will most economically reduce complexity. All such social engineering is doomed to multiply the problems it seeks to resolve for the single reason that it precludes the rationally motivated engagement of all the participants. And so Habermas's answer to critics who want to forcibly impose their structures on our future is, of course, that this only increases our burdens by adding to the pressure of the 'system' on the 'lifeworld'. (I sympathize with the reader who is still finding these concepts impossibly awkward!).

Emancipation can only be achieved through *democracy* and a regeneration of the public sphere — and that is just what the best of the new social movements achieve for us all. Nor should we fall back into the mistake of confusing democracy with its formal structures (representative bodies, parliaments, constitutions, elections, unions and other formal arrangements). Democracy means all that is done 'in' and 'through' communicative interaction, through action that is genuinely 'oriented to reaching an understanding' — Habermas allows for compromises between strategic actors but he treats agreements of this type as secondary or even parasitic forms of association that depend ultimately on the achievements of communicative action. In short, we should think of democracy as a *process of shared learning*.

Those more militant critics who have not heeded the lessons that are to be drawn from the 'engineered' socialism of Eastern Europe always elicit from Habermas the same cautionary admonition. 'Every intervention in complex social structures has such unforeseeable consequences that processes of reform can only be defended as scrupulous processes of trial and error, under the careful control of those who have to bear their consequences' [6]. Some of these critics still pursue Habermas with the argument, cast within his own terms, that communicative action presupposes the very kind of equality and mutuality among the interacting participants that it is supposed to achieve. Habermas responds with the sometimes less than adequate answer that the mutuality is already guaranteed, if only in an anticipatory way, in the very structures of communication, and, further, that in any case the individual always resists total absorption in the system. But what should I *do* in an interaction with another individual who has power over me and who is hell-bent on relating to me only as a strategic actor and in terms solely of his own purposes? We need only generalize the question to see the problem. What do *we* do about *them* (Reagan and his Marines and bankers, who so much want to make us 'free') when *they* relate to *us* only as instruments for *their* purposes? We are met here with Habermas's resolute silence. We must hope that 'Reason without Revolution' [7] will prevail.

FINALLY...

It remains to be seen whether Habermas's theory will work its way into the theoretical and methodological foundations of the several disciplines that it so obviously addresses — anthropology, political science, philosophy, history, the humanities and many others. That is what Habermas's forebears in the 'old' Frankfurt School accomplished in the years before and after the war to the early 1970s. Habermas has used all his brilliance and scholarship to take his readers beyond his own views and into carefully established new points of reference within classical texts that he has brought to life in so many strikingly new perspectives. He has established new foundations and this together with the enormous scope of the theory bode well for its future. Already the work is leading important debates, about art, on the State, and on the nature of modernity — and that is just the beginning.

Not long ago Habermas commented: 'I know that all learning depends on the formation of inner motives' [8]. According to his philosophical theses the inner motive that we all share is the need to better understand our own lives so that we can live together more productively. And inasmuch as his sociological theses are correct, then the course of our present circumstances will make this need ever more immediately and explicitly manifest. Whether or not we find 'answers' in Habermas's theory is for each reader to determine for his or herself. Each will find parts of his work that are impenetrable or unacceptable. But all will find a theory that joins the inner world of our shared subjectivity with the object world 'out there' and, further, an ordered set of concepts and arguments with which to fathom our own social nature and its possibilities. We may not accept what we read, but who dares ask a single scholar to offer more?

NOTES

[1] 'The Dialectics of Rationalisation: An interview with Jürgen Habermas', by Axel Honneth, *et al. Telos*, **49** (Fall), 1981, p. 27.

[2] Habermas, in Honneth interview, p. 28 (see note [1]).

[3] Tom McCarthy discusses these matters in his chapter, 'Reflections on Rationalization in the Theory of Communicative Action', in *Habermas and Modernity*, R. J. Bernstein (ed.), Polity Press, Cambridge, 1985. See also Habermas's reply in the same volume, esp. pp. 204–205.

[4] Habermas, 'Questions and Counterquestions', in *Habermas and Modernity*, p. 192 (see note [3]).

[5] The title of the second volume of the *Theory of Communicative Action (Zur Kritik der funktionalistischen Vernunft)*.

[6] Jürgen Habermas, 'A Philosophico-Political Profile', *New Left Review*, **151**, pp. 75–105, p. 104.

[7] The title of Anthony Gidden's review in *Habermas and Modernity*, pp. 95–124 (see note [3]).

[8] In the Honneth interview, p. 28 (see note [1]).

Further reading

MAJOR WORKS IN ENGLISH TRANSLATION

Towards a Rational Society. Student Protest, Science, and Politics, trans. J. J. Shapiro, Boston: Beacon Press, 1971; London: Heinemann, 1971.

Knowledge and Human Interests, trans. J. J. Shapiro, Boston: Beacon Press, 1971; London: Heinemann, 1972.

Theory and Practice, trans. J. Viertel, Boston: Beacon Press, 1973, London: Heinemann, 1974.

Legitimation Crisis, translated and introduced by T. McCarthy, Boston: Beacon Press, 1975; London: Heinemann, 1976.

Communication and the Evolution of Society, translated and introduced by T. McCarthy, Boston: Beacon Press, 1979; London: Heinemann, 1979.

Reason and the Rationalisation of Society, translated and introduced by T. McCarthy, Boston: Beacon Press, 1984; London: Heinemann, 1984 (the first of two volumes of the *The Theory of Communicative Action*. The second volume *Zur Kritik der funktionalistischen Vernunft* is scheduled to appear in McCarthy's translation and with his introduction in 1987.)

Philosophical–Political Profiles, trans. Frederick G. Lawrence, Cambridge, Mass: MIT Press, 1983; London: Heinemann, 1984.

Lectures on Modernity, currently (1987) in process of translation by T. McCarthy (under this or a similar title).

SELECTED SECONDARY SOURCES

There are now available quite a few books on Habermas and critical theory. For the non-specialist three are especially useful. Thomas McCarthy's book, *The Critical Theory of Jürgen Habermas*, MIT Press, Cambridge, Mass., and London, 1978, deals very clearly with all but Habermas's latest works and does so in a way that stays close to the structure of Habermas's work. The second edition of this title has an extensive bibliography of Habermas's work.

A more general introduction is David Held's very good, *Introduction to Critical Theory; Horkheimer to Habermas*. Hutchinson, London, 1980. This work also contains a useful bibliography.

For the slightly more advanced reader there are two excellent books that present some of Habermas's debates with his critics (on a broad range of central topics) together with clear general introductions to his work. One is *Habermas: Critical Debates*, edited by John B. Thompson and David Held, Macmillan, London, 1982. The second is *Habermas and Modernity*, edited and introduced by Richard J. Bernstein, Polity Press, Cambridge, 1985. Both of these titles deal with the newer writings up to the mid-1980s, including Habermas's major work (*The Theory of Communicative Action*). Bernstein's introduction is perhaps the best short non-specialized introduction to Habermas's work that is available.

SOME SUGGESTIONS ON HOW TO READ HABERMAS

The beginner reader who wants to grasp Habermas through his more *philosophically oriented writings* should begin with the appendix of *Knowledge and Human Interests* (not the postscript) and then read Bernstein's introduction to *Habermas and Modernity*. After this, several other reasonably accessible courses into the work are open. One route that leads through Habermas's earlier basic arguments against positivism, 'scientism', and ideology, can be 'reconstructed' by reading the very accessible Chapters 4 and 5 of *Towards a Rational Society* and then the first and, especially, the last chapters of *Theory and Practice*. The mature result of this work is to be found in Chapters 1 and 4 of *Reason and the Rationalisation of Society*.

The recent title *Philosophical-Political Profiles* is comparatively easy to read, but it is not systematic and is distanced from Habermas's main sociological theses.

For the reader who is particularly interested in Habermas's engagement with *philosophical hermeneutics* and his dialogue with Gadamer it would be useful to read part three of H. G. Gadamer's, *Truth and Method*, and Habermas's review of that work that is available in *Understanding Social Inquiry*, F. R. Dallmayr and T. A. McCarthy (eds), University of Notre Dame Press, 1977. Gadamer's defence of his own positions is available in H. G. Gadamer 'On the Scope and Function of Hermeneutical Reflection', *Continuum*, **8**, 8, 1970. See also the excellent discussion, 'Ethics and

Culture: Habermas and Gadamer in Dialogue' by Paul Ricoeur, *Philosophy Today*, **17**, No. 2/4 Summer 1973.

The reader who wants to take the quickest route into the political sociology should begin, as must every reader, with the appendix (not the postscript) to *Knowledge and Human Interests* and proceed from there to the now dated but still accessible and important last chapter of *Towards a Rational Society*. The next easy step is to the extract from *Legitimation Crisis* that is available as 'What does a Crisis Mean Today? Legitimation Problems in late Capitalism', *Social Research*, **40**, 1973. A somewhat changed version of the earlier political sociology is offered in the last chapter of *Communication and the Evolution of Society*. This course then leads to Chapter 4 of *Reason and the Rationalisation of Society* and, thereafter, into the arguments of the second volume of the *Theory of Communicative Action*.

The reader who is especially interested in the *theory of communication* should look in the the appendix of *Knowledge and Human Interests* and Chapter 10 of that work for the context of Habermas's first very important notion of 'Systematically Distorted Communication' that is to be found in *Inquiry*, No. 13, 1970. This leads to another basic formulation, 'What is Universal Pragmatics' that is offered as the first chapter of *Communication and the Evolution of Society*. The way is then open to Chapter 3 of *Reason and the Rationalisation of Society*.

Index